WHAT WOULD APPLE DO?

D1428268

Dirk Beckmann

WHAT WOULD APPLE DO?

How you can learn from
Apple and make money

Inspirations and ideas

Translated and adapted from
German by David B. Jones

Biteback Publishing

First published in Great Britain in 2013 by
Biteback Publishing Ltd
Westminster Tower
3 Albert Embankment
London SE1 7SP
Copyright © Dirk Beckmann 2013

First published in Germany in 2011 as Was würde Apple tun?
by Econ Verlag, a division of Ullstein Buchverlage GmbH

Dirk Beckmann has asserted his right under the Copyright, Designs and
Patents Act 1988 to be identified as the author of this work.

ISBN 978-1-84954-573-0

10 9 8 7 6 5 4 3 2 1

A CIP catalogue record for this book is available from the
British Library.

Set in Chronicle and Helvetica Neue

Printed and bound in Great Britain by
CPI Group (UK) Ltd, Croydon CR0 4YY

MIX
Paper from
responsible sources
FSC® C020471

CONTENTS

AUTHOR'S NOTE

This book is not meant to be a technical work and it is not an insider story. I am not connected to Apple in any way, and have neither worked for Apple nor received any payment or gratification.

I have a blog (*www.what-would-apple-do.com*) on which I post occasional interesting pieces of news regarding this book and Apple in general.

Dirk Beckmann
June 2013

PREFACE

When I started work on the German version of this book in 2010, the iPad had just been launched. Steve Jobs was at the peak of his creativity and Apple had not quite yet become the most valuable listed company in the world.

With the iPad, Apple pulled off a coup that equalled or even surpassed the launch of the Macintosh in 1984. With the iPad, Apple heralded the post-PC era. Of course, the device was at first ridiculed by industry experts. But Apple already had the market clout to convince its customers – practically overnight – that when it came to writing emails, reading or surfing the Net, the cumbersome PC had had its day.

Now, in mid-2013, the world has changed yet again. Apple is the world's most valuable listed company and Steve Jobs is no longer with us. The market has been flooded with books about the Apple founder, among them a particularly worthwhile biography by Walter Isaacson.

In the last two years, Apple has not been able to herald any new revolution comparable to the creation of the post-PC era, and has concentrated instead on consolidating its market dominance. Some experts claim that Apple has become a 'supply chain company': a firm that knows how to design desirable products, produce them cheaply in the Far East and sell them at an inflated price.

In the final quarter of 2012, Apple made around $1 billion profit per week, but was still punished by the stock exchanges. Despite growth in sales, the share price fell at an alarming rate. Steve Wozniak, the co-founder of the organisation, was already warning that

Apple must be careful not to lose its 'cool factor' as a brand.

More than once in the thirty-plus years of its existence, Apple has been pronounced dead. Now, once again, the company has a great opportunity to prove otherwise. Despite declining popularity among the so-called multipliers, early adopters and evangelists, and what hard-core fans saw as disappointing product presentations in the last two years – the company's latest innovations failing to match the calibre of the iPad – Apple is in the pole position and is still capable of revolutionising a number of markets. This is particularly true for the television market, if the numerous rumours about an Apple TV are to be believed.

No matter what the people at Cupertino in California are conjuring up at the moment, the developments are always exciting to follow, especially if you are an entrepreneur wondering how to deal with the digital shift.

Following the German first edition, I have revised this book extensively, leaving out

Google and other competitors to concentrate exclusively on Apple.

The text is deliberately short and focused. If there's one thing you can learn from Apple, it's to focus on what's really important and to leave out the rest.

The first section of this book highlights three areas where you can learn from Apple: Apple has a special mindset, a unique way of doing things, and sells its innovative products by means of what is probably the best communication strategy in the corporate world.

The second section demonstrates how Apple methods can be applied to other industries. If the Apple mindset, development methods and communication strategy were to be used to create, for example, an automobile, it would be different to anything ever seen before. A kitchen would function in a completely different way and toys would provide a whole host of new possibilities to both parents and children.

This book is aimed at anyone who wants to develop their products or services and position themselves in the digital market. It is intended for all people who face the question of how to realign their products, services, processes and communication for the digital age.

INTRODUCTION

All received wisdom would say that there's no way Apple could be successful because it completely ignores conventional business practices. It serves a wide variety of different markets and operates in a proprietary, integrated technical world. The investment in R&D is mind-blowing. The employees develop innovations in interdisciplinary teams with an enormous amount of effort, but then go on to find fault after fault in their own ideas. All information about new products is kept top secret (and top secret *means* top secret) right up to the launch. When you think about how little Apple takes ordinary business principles to heart, you realise that any potential investor would normally refuse to give this firm a single dollar.

But Apple doesn't need investors, and it's doing just fine without them. Since 1997, the company has been able to increase its stock value to a higher level than that of Google, Microsoft or Facebook. Since 2011, Apple has been the world's most valuable company. With products such as iTunes, iPod, iPhone and iPad, Apple not only makes an enormous profit, but has also opened up completely new markets.

The Apple system takes markets by storm and represents a combination of modernity, lifestyle and quality. However, the best bit for the company and its shareholders is this: Apple is making money. The company is profitable in every field.

So what makes Apple so successful? The answer used to be: the company is blessed with a charismatic boss who seems to succeed in everything he does. Someone whose keynote speeches are the inspiration for thousands of speakers. Someone who makes one ground-breaking decision after another.

But today we know that Apple is so much more than just Steve Jobs. Apple is a concept. A concept that is well worth learning from because it represents a company with a reputation for overcoming seemingly invincible obstacles to create great new things. A company that chases up seemingly crazy ideas and will not rest until it has put them into action, and which keeps finding new opportunities to make money in the digital world. *Loads* of money – we're talking (in early 2013) about $130 billion in cash.

So what makes Apple the greatest innovator in the digital world right now? How has this company, whose products are shunned by professional users as lifestyle gadgets, and often labelled as too expensive, come to be the most innovative of all technology brands? What have products such as the iPhone or the iPad got that sets them apart from their competitors? What did Apple do to become such a global phenomenon?

The way in which Apple takes business models from the analogue world and modifies them for today's digital world has become another important keystone of its success. It creates new markets using business models that were unthinkable in the old days: a perfect example of digital evolution from a businessman's point of view. The success of iTunes and the iPod was only possible because Apple threw out well-worn mindsets, concentrating instead on putting a brand new business model into action.

While the music industry completely failed to anticipate the digital revolution, Apple decided to talk with the record labels about developing a digital sales system for music. Lengthy discussions and a great deal of persuasion were necessary. But it worked, and today the labels generate a significant share of their income through the world's largest music vendor – Apple. The legal and technical barriers appeared insurmountable and scared everyone else off from even trying to move in the direction that Apple was taking. No one believed that customers would ever go back to paying for something that was available for free and only a few clicks away. Before iTunes, it was practically impossible to purchase music legally from the Internet. Yet today the quick-and-easy-to-buy music files from iTunes are seen as a cheap alternative to the traditional CD. Being able to download individual songs for seventy-nine pence and purchase albums for a standard fixed price has become the norm for the entire music industry.

Like no other company, Apple knows how to get rid of any obstacles standing in the way of a project.

The ever-increasing digitalisation of the world we live and work in poses a number of questions for the future. One of the most important is how to earn money. The book you now have in your hands is intended to inspire you. It explains, from Apple, that you can learn to be successful and earn money from the digital industries.

Apple stands for a digital transformation that retains the established economic way of thinking. In this way, it has every chance of becoming a pioneer providing inspiration for a wide range of business sectors. Anyone can see how single-mindedly it works to design new products and bring them to life. When you pick up an Apple product, you just know it's something special. The reason why Apple is so good at doing what it does is because it strikes the ideal balance between the business model and technology and delivering what the customer wants.

Apple, like no other company, knows how to tap into consumer needs and desires, and this forms the foundation of its success. Yes, Apple does look at the behaviour of its customers. However, unlike most other companies Apple does not rely on market research. It creates products using simple common sense. Apple either concentrates on getting just a few functions completely right, or it creates products that are so incredibly new that they go way beyond just satisfying customer needs.

Apple wants its customers to pay a reasonable price for its products. That's why it develops new digital business models based not only on the new opportunities and requirements of the digital world, but also on its corporate goals. With this approach, Apple can supply products that look great and are easy to use, and also earn the company money.

From its hardware to its software, Apple is simply world class. It understands better than others that technology is at its best when the user doesn't even notice it. After all, accessible appliances are the product not just of coming up with the right concept, but also of employing brilliant technology. Silently doing its job, yet an integral part of the whole.

Companies like Apple have developed an innovation culture which is completely different to that of traditional firms because the entire company is driven by a spirit of inventiveness and not just by the R&D department. Right from the start, ideas have always been the engine for growth in the IT and Internet sectors. But far more important than the idea is how it can be turned into a finished product or service. What processes are necessary? How do the employees identify with it? Not until the idea is so easy and quick to understand that it can speak for itself will it sell successfully. If you can grasp the benefit or advantage of a product in seconds, then you are ready to spend money on it. Apple has taken this concept to heart in its innovation process. That's why its customers are happy to pay more for fewer functions. Of course, these functions do have to be the right ones.

When you want to build up or expand a business it's worth thinking about the way Apple does things, and taking a fresh look at both your new and current products and services with Apple's ideas and concepts in mind.

WHAT YOU
CAN LEARN
FROM APPLE

MINDSET

Apple embodies a unique mindset regarding innovative digital products. Priority is given to focusing on what really matters and on the specific usefulness of a product. In order to achieve results such as the creation of the iPhone, every employee of the company has to adopt this way of thinking. The Apple mindset is the basis on which the whole company operates, because it can provide answers to numerous questions. This mindset can thus be regarded as an element of Apple's corporate identity.

SAYING NO

Apple believes that less is more. Instead of cramming as many features as possible into its products – something which its competitors love to do – Apple *leaves out* as many as possible. It makes products that are easy for the customer to understand. Visions such as the first portable computer, the lightest laptop and a computer with no mouse or keyboard are what drive Apple's product development, not the technical possibilities.

The website *www.apple.com* illustrates this reduction principle particularly well: it starts with just a single message. Although Apple has an enormous need to communicate, the website welcomes the visitor with a few simple navigation points and a starting page without clutter. No shouting, no flashing lights, hardly any animations. The minimalist structure of the website concentrates on one particular product, drawing our attention, for example, to the new iPod generation or a new version of iTunes. For years, this site has had a reputation for being an inspiration to web designers and it is the template for numerous Internet presences.

If, for example, you want to build the lightest portable computer, there are problems that have to be solved. The MacBook Air offers a radical example of Apple being prepared to say no. The CD drive contained in all computers until this point was too big and too heavy to be part of the lightest laptop. Despite every user needing one from time to time, the lightest computer could only be produced without a CD drive. So a technology was created with which CD drives – usually available in other computers – could be accessed via a network. Anyone travelling with a MacBook Air who meets up with another Apple user can use this person's CD drive. So it's possible to install programs and load music from CDs without having to carry the necessary device around with you. A lesser firm than Apple would simply have included a CD drive and would have missed out on something completely unique: the world's thinnest and lightest laptop.

Saying no demonstrates the art of taking decisions right at the development stage, and avoids confusing the customer with no end of settings and options. Saying no also means continually asking the question: 'Is this thing really necessary?'

Developing something simple therefore means doing without various things. But today, leaving things out is not considered particularly innovative – quite the opposite in fact. In business, politics and science the rule is always 'the more the better'.

With this in mind, it's a risky business offering less than one's competitors. Simply leaving out possible functions, new product attributes and features does not seem to bear the hallmarks of a successful business plan. And why should it? It's easy to follow the example of Microsoft Word and equip a text processing program with every function ever invented; it doesn't mean you have to use them all. You can develop a website that displays its complete contents on one hopelessly cluttered start page. But this does not guarantee accessible products that are easy to use. Quite the opposite. Far too many gadgets are crammed so full of functions that not even a weighty manual will make them easier to understand.

Very rarely do people want everything at the same time. Their way of life normally means that they prefer using the perfect product or service for the situation at hand. So which products do people recommend? And which ones really win the hearts of their customers? The answer is clear: the ones that are wonderfully simple.

Apple followed this path religiously with the iPhone and its applications. The telephone basically consists of hardware and an operating system called iOS on which applications (apps) run. One of these apps allows you to make telephone calls. Another shows you the weather. Yet another lets you play videos and so on. This method of dividing things up into smaller specialised applications has inspired thousands of developers to work in a more focused way. In fact, it shook up the whole industry and numerous imitations rapidly appeared.

In his book *ReWork,* Jason Fried tells the reader: 'Underdo your competitor.' And he adds: 'Conventional wisdom says that to beat your competitors, you need to one-up them. If they have four features, you need five, or fifteen, or twenty-five. If they're spending $20,000, you need to spend $30,000. If they have fifty employees, you need a hundred.' He tells us that, on the other hand, doing *less* means fewer functions, fewer options and defaults, fewer people or simpler structures in an organisation, fewer meetings, less abstract thinking and fewer promises.

Fried is an Apple fan. He learned from

Apple, developed his own ideas, and built up 37signals, a successful firm selling web-based software with relatively few employees. He installs the *right* features, not just everything that's possible in the hope that some of it will suit the user's requirements.

Software that provides an enormous number of options is made by developers who hate making decisions and can't say no. You need a lot more courage to leave something out than to add something in. Deciding which options are the right ones is not an easy task.

And there are also the demands of customers and colleagues from other departments to consider. Everyone seems to want something different. The world is full of football coaches: everyone seems to think they know best. Customers tend to come up with things like, 'What use is a product without this function? How on earth can you work with this or benefit from it?' Yet *someone* has to decide which needs should be satisfied and which features should be left out. Someone has to say no.

We live in an age in which the thousands of opportunities available to us make us want to take advantage of them all. It is, however, important to realise that this multitude of possibilities makes it all the more important to concentrate on what really matters.

BEING PRAGMATIC

Apple thinks around current business models and customer habits and boldly continues to enhance them. In this regard, the international corporation resembles a simple mid-sized company. Apple shows a spirit of inventiveness and a passion for quality by focusing on creating products that are geared to the basic needs of its customers – just as a mid-sized company does.

With the iPad, Apple remained true to its principles. When this innovative gadget was presented in 2010, the 'professionals' tore it apart. No one needs something that's basically a cross between a computer and a smartphone, they said. It does not solve any real problem, technically it's nothing special, there are no real features; basically, it's not going to be a success.

And yet practically all Apple products are successful, because like the iPad they focus on the needs of normal people. The company's numerous imitators have until now only been able to compete by indulging in fierce price wars.

Apple shows us that there *is* a way to digital success. If you want to tread this path then you have to be prepared to break the rules of the respective markets. This involves not only offering innovative products and services but also taking into account current realities: realities that result from people wanting to use technology without having to be an expert. On the Internet, earning money with closed systems like Apple is not particularly popular. However, a total free-for-all and a completely open Net can often get in the way of any value being created. Apple succeeds in selling the idea of a product to the customer quickly and directly. The Apple product is attractive, feels good in your hand, and is simple. If, following this initial emotional experience, the customer is still undecided as to which device to purchase, Apple can also offer rational selling points such as outstanding performance data and unique functions.

Apple's trick is to manufacture products with benefits that any customer can grasp immediately.

Product development is solely about ordinary people and their ordinary needs.

SOLVING PROBLEMS

With the appearance of file-sharing on the Internet at the end of the 1990s, buying music on CD became less and less attractive to young consumers. Equipped with an MP3 player and a PC, they could download music legally from the Internet and share it with friends. There was a time when many young people carried hard drives full of music and films around with them so that their friends could make a copy. This resulted in sales falling dramatically for many retailers and producers, which led to a complete transformation of the music industry. When Apple came up with a system for the legal purchase of digital music, the iTunes Music Store, and an appropriate player, the iPod, it was too late for some music publishers.

Yet a product like music is perfect for the digital age: you can copy it easily, you can sell it in small units and you can enjoy it immediately. Unlike a sofa or a packet of muesli, a song or album can be consumed straight away. After making a digital purchase there's no long wait for the delivery.

Whether the debate is over music, software, films or books, today's media managers have been the subject of enormous criticism. They have been called backward and lacking in vision because they had absolutely no idea what to do about the culture of free downloading. In the early 2000s, the music industry did not see any future in selling digital music, so Apple was able to move into that gap. The biggest music trader in the world today found a new customer-friendly way to sell digital music and was thus able to charge for a service that had previously been free.

How did they achieve this? Instead of asking thousands of music-loving downloaders what they wanted, Apple started to develop ideas of its own. And that's how the company found a gap in the market: providing digital music legally for people who just wanted to listen to music – no more, no less. People who were not bothered whether songs were 'tagged' or whether they were digitalised at the right resolution. In order to put the idea into action, Apple was prepared to tread a stony path: entering into difficult negotiations with the music industry, developing completely new software, designing attractive new devices and painstakingly putting them all together to create a functioning unit. Finally, iTunes was born: a novel ecosystem with a perfect product for music lovers with money to spend.

CDs, printed newspapers and books have an inbuilt copy protection mechanism or at least carry a notice regarding illegal reproduction, because they only exist in time and space. So how can you sell a text, an article or a song today when a copy of it can be made and sent around the world in milliseconds? Answering that question is one of the most important tasks for the future. Only when it is solved can new media work successfully for the entire business world and its stakeholders.

No matter how the question about copyright protection is answered, one thing is certain: to earn money from ideas and products today, you have to target normal consumers. One important success formula is therefore to make complicated things simple and to reach a broad target group in order to generate profit. This may involve regulation, product protection and holding back on new technical developments.

If you want people to pay for your digital products and services, you have to create products that are good value and can serve a real purpose.

A successful product has to solve a specific problem; for instance how to download and listen to music without having to worry about the technology.

CULTIVATING INVENTIVENESS

Some manufacturers let their customers develop the products by handing over customer support to enthusiastic users. It's known as crowdsourcing and involves getting users to help solve corporate tasks and problems. Advocates of this outsourcing concept claim that the masses are smarter than individual experts and can therefore create better products and content. Of course there are those who think differently, for example Nicolas Carr. He describes web 2.0 as a 'dictatorship of amateurs'.

Crowdsourcing is very much in vogue. The trend of letting customers take part in product development or product configuration is discussed at conferences dedicated entirely to the subject. Everywhere you hear people describing this phenomenon as the democratisation of product development and the ultimate success model for the future.

Apple, on the other hand, trusts its own experts. At Apple, it is the highly qualified technicians, designers and strategists who think up new products. This is because the company does not want to surrender its responsibility for product development. Traditional companies probably find it hard to understand what's so special about this because mid-sized machine manufacturers, for example, have always worked this way.

However, a company taking its first tentative steps in the digital world will soon be surrounded by advisers, preaching the new principles of the Internet. The motto is always: 'Get your customers inventing, writing, thinking, helping...' The new world of the 'involved' masses sounds great, but it's not sustainable. People *love* being able to participate. However, developing a concept is still hard work. And if you want someone to write that perfect professional text then you're probably going to have to pay them for it. And more importantly, why should users pay for something they can do themselves? Most people are only ready to part with money if they feel they're getting a valuable service in return.

A company is not going to be a success in the digital sector by asking the masses to come up with new ideas, write texts or make films. The way forward is to define a clear product selling point or develop an unmistakable design. And this must be part of a business model that works for both the manufacturer and the customer. Henry Ford knew this and is quoted as saying: 'If I'd asked my customers what they wanted, they'd have said faster horses.'

Microsoft, for example, has often been criticised in the past for having software that resembles a banana: it's still ripening when the customer buys it. However, now that the commercial Internet has become more and more successful, and customer participation extremely popular, 'banana products' are all the rage.

Anyone who wants to generate sustainable digital profit has to remember that the paying customer expects fully functional products of the highest quality. Customers want to unwrap their purchase or click on it and use it straight away. They want to write a text, edit a film, or play a game. What they *don't* want to do is pay for an unfinished product.

Of course, Apple is also interested in customer feedback and builds it into the product development process. But it still carries out the bulk of the work itself and doesn't try to delegate tasks to others. Returning to Henry Ford's example, we see that Apple is always building something new, like that first car, while others are just busy trying to develop better carriages drawn by faster horses.

Apple doesn't ask its customers about what they want: it simply relies on its savvy employees to come up with remarkable product.

A PASSION FOR DETAIL

Michael Lopp, a former Apple developer, claims that Apple excels in producing 'really good ideas wrapped up in other really good ideas'. In other words, a successful Apple product is the result of a great deal of effort and numerous optimisations in all areas of the company. These include not only the development of the devices, the packaging of the accessories, and those famous ads, but also the email that reaches the customer who has written a complaint in the online shop.

To ensure that every employee goes to work with the same positive attitude, identical innovation processes must be used in all areas of the company. If a company always uses the same process to evaluate new ideas for production or marketing, it can use this to develop new ideas within new ideas and comprehensively optimise them.

This attention to detail can be seen at Apple in every area. Great products with beautiful packaging are sold in uniquely designed stores. In the physical store, the customer experiences the Apple way of doing things, not only through trying out the many devices on display, but also because the shop itself has been well planned right down to the last detail. The mobile cash desks, for example, are small devices that allow the customer to pay without leaving the display area. In this way, Apple saves the customers from having to wait at the checkout and surprises them with yet another welcome detail.

Delegating the innovation process to the R&D department means that while you *will* get ideas for new products, you then have the cumbersome task of selling them to the other departments, or marketing them using the same old clichés. Apple relies on carrying out research and development throughout the company, and thus ensures the attention to detail for which it is famous. The purchasing department has to search for new ways of doing things, as do the controlling and production departments. To achieve this, a constant exchange of ideas regarding the goal and the resources needed to achieve it is crucial. After all, a purchasing officer who only judges a supplier by the price would probably have decided against the white earphones that have become the trademark of the iPod.

If the production department simply follows commercial trends and purchases enormous machines that can do almost anything, the products will probably end up with more features than necessary – in an attempt to justify the large investment. If someone in project management is on the lookout for new ways of handling projects that are becoming more and more complex, the result will probably involve procedures that lead to long running times and increased expenditure. It is therefore important that a company clearly defines its innovation philosophy and implements it universally.

Most companies, however, fail to meet this challenge. Senior management often makes the mistake of asking the IT department to develop solutions for the digital revolution. The main responsibilities of an IT department are usually: managing the company's IT systems, developing individual software and supporting employees with technical problems. The Internet, however, is more than just new technology. The business model and user orientation have to be considered, and this is not normally a task for IT administrators, who tend to decide on a product, choose a system integrator and then roll out a lengthy project using tried and tested IT procedures. What eventually appears on the Internet is very rarely an innovative digital product that can hold its own against the global competition.

Only when all the relevant departments have understood that the innovation process concerns everyone, and is not just the responsibility of the boss, R&D, or an external service provider, can a great idea turn into a ground-breaking product.

Only when you devote as much attention to the minor details as to the major features can you turn an average product into something exceptional.

BEING THE BEST

The speed at which innovations and new Internet trends appear is sending a clear message: it's now or never! However, Apple's experience in recent years has shown that you don't have to be the first at something to earn money from it.

Changes in the digital world require many businesses to rethink their strategy. Markets which exist today may be gone tomorrow. Even modern companies such as Nokia, once the undisputed market leader in mobile phones, are facing enormous challenges; the battle for mobile domination is currently being fought out between other technology companies from outside the sector, such as

Google and Apple. But few people would dare to write Nokia off quite yet. With their experience and professionalism, such firms may well have the capacity to regain momentum.

While on the one hand it is important to find new ways to develop innovations, on the other hand companies need secure structures that ensure they don't blindly follow every trend and end up losing any clear focus. One rule that you can learn from Apple is: it's not important to be first; it's important to be *better*.

Despite the speed at which trends and innovations emerge, the first on the market does not necessarily have the best chance of success. More important is finding the *right* moment to launch one's digital products and services using the right business model.

On the Internet, *first* is not automatically *best*. Companies that are quick *and* good will most likely have no problem creating a profitable digital future. But those who just launch a product quickly, hoping that the customers will help to make it good, may just see their digital reputation go up in smoke. Sometimes it may be necessary to occupy a market with quick solutions, but normally what customers want are good products. Those who try to achieve too much too soon run the risk of failure. Trying to be quick combined with a lack of experience can lead people to make over-hasty decisions. Unfinished test versions are often launched just to make their existence known; and when they flop, it's the fault of the Internet, the user or someone else.

If a company can see what works well and what doesn't by looking at its competitors' products, then it can be innovative without investing too much money. The subject matter can be carefully examined in-house and the necessary conclusions drawn. When the company has found out how to be better than its competitors, a professionally developed product with a modern business model will attract customers, despite being a latecomer to the market.

Apple's product development has a clear strategic focus: quality and originality. The company took the risk of investing an estimated $150 million in developing the iPhone – a product for an already established market. At that time, larger companies with considerably more experience dominated the market. But Apple was confident enough to enter the ring, and quickly became one of the largest producers of smartphones. It was able to solve many problems experienced by the customers of the market pioneers, and these solutions became the decisive selling points for the iPhone.

This phenomenon can also be seen with other Apple products. While the whole world was speculating about when Apple would finally address the trend towards affordable netbooks, the people in Cupertino declared that they were not interested in this market. However, in 2010 the iPad – Apple's unique combination of mobile phone, e-book reader and PC – finally appeared.

Apple also took its time developing the iPad, looking carefully at what its competitors were up to and what the customers were really doing with their devices. Which problems were worth solving? And what markets could be opened up? By integrating several aspects of user behaviour such as media consumption, online surfing, sending emails and using apps, and combining this with the successful app store, a product was created that went on to become the template for a brand new market segment.

Even when faced with dominant market leaders, it is possible to launch successful products late in the day. Nothing has to remain as it is. In today's digital world, the fact that Google is one of the world's most valuable companies is less significant than it would have been back in the analogue days, because Internet users are more willing to change their service provider. This would suggest that Microsoft's alternative search engine Bing is not automatically doomed to failure just because everyone is using Google at the moment. With a new leader like Marissa Mayer, even Yahoo! may be able to recover its old strengths.

Not having to be first does not mean, however, sitting back and taking things easy, or waiting to see what happens. Good digital products require time and investment. You need a team, good suppliers and a perfect internal structure. Setting up these resources, creating products and testing and improving them is an important and urgent task. Only once challenges have been identified during the development stage can they be faced effectively.

To design outstanding products, it is essential to have enough time at your disposal. That's why being the first doesn't necessarily mean being the best.

TAKING CONTROL

One of the main reasons for the success of the Internet and the way in which it has spread like wildfire is the open nature of its technology. The underlying technical structures are, for the most part, freely accessible. And for many, openness and free access to information – the founding principles of the Internet – are seen as basic human rights. Restrictions of any kind are frowned upon.

However, since the end of the last century, many directors and managers have made the mistake of including technical openness in their business models, offering free online access to their products. Now the companies are surprised that customers are not willing to pay for many of the services offered on the web. And nothing can really be said against an infrastructure with open technology, equally accessible to all.

But in the past ten years, it has often been claimed that openness towards customers would be rewarded. All you had to do was let the customer take part in product development, customer service or the pricing process, and success would come automatically. As proof, the story is often told of the architects who didn't know where to build the paths on a university campus. First they chose not to build any at all, and when it came to laying the asphalt they simply used the tracks left by students on the grass as a blueprint. The message here is: the people are the real experts ('The wisdom of the crowd'). However, involving the customer or user also has its downside. Deciding how streets are best laid out is a question for professionals. After all, architects go to college to learn that sort of thing. A campus based on what the students want right now is not going to work in the long run. What's going to happen if it starts to snow or if a fire breaks out?

Journalism offers another example. If you really want to understand something correctly, you will probably still put your faith in a newspaper – despite this being the age of open debate and citizen journalism. Only a journalist or blogger whose reputation and career depend on accurate reports will take the necessary care to back up all his information with sources. It's hard work being professional. The current crisis in the world of newspapers, and in the music and film industries, are further examples of what can happen when people misunderstand openness.

Theoretically, the technical basics of the Internet can provide you with everything you need to fulfil your dreams. Anyone can create a website, for example. Anyone can start their own radio station and no longer be forced to listen to whatever the media companies blast them with.

Anyone?

The web, with its open systems, will *not*

automatically lead to more democratic structures. Why? Because the number of people who really understand open technology and can therefore use it is remarkably small. A theoretical *could* is completely different from a practical *can*.

Most people are not able to program HTML pages so that they can be found by search engines. Many have no idea why a search result appears with a particular ranking and believe that's just the way it is. Only a few can install the latest version of the Linux open-source operating system – an open system that is continuously being improved by developers around the world – on a PC. And using free software such as Open Office, or setting up a blog on one's own web server, is not everyone's thing. It is often argued that these 'dummies' are a dying species: people who are simply too old to understand the new world and play an active role in it. Yet it's the younger generation of 'digital natives', who have grown up with new media, who often do not really understand what they're doing on the Internet and use, for example, Facebook without having any idea of what happens to all their data. Later, when they apply for a job, they are often surprised how much can be found out about them on the Internet.

Even though the Net *does* offer many new opportunities to express oneself, this doesn't mean that everyone is able to make use of them. You could even say that freedom and openness – considered by many to be the fundamental principles of the Internet and which have led to the existence of numerous free technologies – may actually be a major obstacle for the majority of people who are not on the Internet day and night.

And this is where Apple comes in.

With the iPad, for example, Apple invented a new category of computer and created a brand new market, not for technology professionals, but for a society getting tired of putting one folder into another. A society that doesn't understand why you have to press 'Start' to switch off the computer. Thanks to the iPad, anyone can take part in the digital revolution. Many older people, who in the past would rarely dare to try to use a PC, can now hardly imagine being without their iPads. Using the data included in an app can certainly take some getting used to. But thanks to the lack of a general data system, the complexity is considerably reduced. Desktop software uses a complicated file system, on which it is possible to open files with the wrong software. This is not the case with the iPad, on which each app can only access the appropriate files, making the device infinitely more user friendly.

Of course, it *is* possible to criticise the closed nature of the Apple system. But anyone who wants to utilise Apple's basic principle of simplification in order to reach people must be prepared to make compromises.

Integrated systems allow us to maintain control over the user experience, thus ensuring that anyone can use the product without difficulty.

PRODUCT DEVELOPMENT

Apple nurtures a unique mindset regarding innovation and has, over the years, installed an equally unique development model. This has arisen from the spirit of the last thirty years and revolves around a method called 'Design Thinking'. Apple is the pioneer in this discipline and is cited in countless books as the prime example of the new way of thinking in product development.

THINKING LIKE A DESIGNER

'Design Thinking' is a term that crops up again and again when you read about Apple. It describes a method for developing innovative ideas that involves regularly bringing together all the important stakeholders in multidisciplinary teams. 'Working like a designer' means that new things are created and then rejected. Then something else is created and rejected. This carries on until a solution is found that is accessible to all.

The founder of the Institute of Design at Stanford University puts it like this: 'Designers have methodical experience from which all members of a multidisciplinary team can learn. Design Thinking holds the team together and makes it successful.'

Many people think in this way, one of the best known among them being Tim Brown, founder and owner of the design hotshop IDEO. Mark Hurst, the adviser and conference organiser who approaches the topic using 'User Experience', and SAP founder Hasso Plattner, who established Design Thinking as a higher education course at his HPI School in Potsdam, also belong to this school of thought.

Although the way in which the Design Thinking method is described varies somewhat depending on the institution, three factors have emerged which are common to all:

- Observing the user is the most important starting point for these studies. This is in stark contrast to the analytical method in which the developer uses market research, statistics and customer surveys.

- The ideas are developed in the multidisciplinary teams described before, using an *iterative* process.
- This method then involves the building of *prototypes* to make the ideas tangible and practicable so that an excellent basis for decision-making can be achieved.

Like the iterative approach, this method is all about the user. The product development process does not focus on surveys or target group analyses but rather on the users and their specific situations. The analysis centres on so-called touchpoints: points at which the customer comes into contact with products. You can have contact with an automobile manufacturer, for example, in various ways: via advertising, in a newspaper report, at the car dealer, as a passenger in a car, on the Internet, as a mechanic and so on. This procedure provides us with important information about the future customer. One important rule is not to ask about the user's opinions, but to observe them with an open mind and draw your own conclusions from what you see.

Tom Klinkowstein, a New York professor of design and new media, compares Design Thinking to Business Thinking as follows:

Business Thinking	Design Thinking
Market analysis	What *might* be
Definitive	Iterative
Focus groups	Observation
Spreadsheets	Scenarios
Individual responsibility	Collaboration
Permanent jobs	Temporary projects

For traditional companies, Design Thinking may sound like something that's nice to have but not necessary. Many companies regard design as nothing more than 'beautification' – an attitude which can have devastating results in the digital age.

The way forward for anyone who wants to survive in the digital world is to develop user-oriented solutions employing iterative and interdisciplinary methods. Why? Because things have become so much more complex. In the past, you had only to keep your eye on a comparatively simple market, on the competition and the technology typical of the particular sector. In the ever-changing world of the Internet, this is no longer so. Addressing this in the classical way, using linear procedures and rigid information and communication structures, can only lead to one thing: failure.

To develop brilliant products and services, you and your colleagues have to find a balance between the business model, user interests and technology. To do this you need to create a culture that requires your staff to contribute ideas and follow up on them as a team. No one can create a product like the iPhone on their own.

Jonathan Ive works together with a small team of talented designers; he creates things, rejects them and has prototypes built which are then constantly improved upon. The designers talk to the finance people and the engineers. And after this first round, they start again from scratch. The iterative procedure has a beginning, but no pre-determined end, apart from the agreed deadline. We're talking about a process where an idea that just a moment ago seemed brilliant can be dropped for a new and even better one.

To work in this way it is crucial that everyone communicates. It is therefore important to introduce or intensify a real communication culture. After all, ideas generated by individuals will only get the essential quality checks if they are communicated to colleagues. On the other hand, the classical top-down strategy favoured by most companies will only lead to monolithic solutions, not innovations.

So we see that Design Thinking requires a new culture and a new entrepreneurial spirit. People who continue talking about problems, not solutions, who lose sight of the vision as soon as an obstacle arises and who wait for their superiors to make decisions, can forget about coming up with new products that will cause a real stir and sell millions.

Apple captured this spirit in 1997 in the stirring promotional film 'Think Different'. This commercial sings the praises of lateral thinkers, freaks and non-conformists. It was the ad that rewrote advertising history when it was shown during the Super Bowl, and which not only moved Apple firmly into the spotlight – where the brand has remained ever since – but also highlighted the way forward within the company: be different, look for different ways of doing things and pursue them religiously.

To carry out the product development process like a designer means observing customers in multidisciplinary teams, developing ideas iteratively and evaluating these ideas using prototypes.

OBSERVING

Everyone will recognise the following situation: a group of people meet up one evening to enjoy a glass of wine and solve the world's problems. If you listen in, you will hear discussions in which the views expressed are mainly personal ones. Each point of view will often also be influenced by the occasion, the place or the other people present. Perhaps one of those present wants to impress the others with his knowledge, while another wants to stand out and so takes an extreme position, with someone else taking an opposing stand.

In the product development process, companies often put their faith in so-called focus groups. These groups are really nothing more than a facilitated version of the group of people just described. This is true, at least, regarding the communication dynamics and the process of forming opinions within groups. Be honest – would you trust this group with a fundamental analysis of a particular market? Would it be a good idea to ask these people whether you should invest millions in a particular strategy?

What we have all experienced and learned in private groups applies just as much to focus groups: there are leaders of the pack whom the others instinctively follow. Yet when the discussion is over, everyone starts behaving independently again. People *say* a lot of things. However, it's what they *do* that's important for business. Some people simply cannot be put into any classical target group: the sort of people who drive their Porsches to a cut-price store, then stay in a budget hotel and later dine in a gourmet restaurant. Consumers are no longer willing just to follow a trend, preferring to comb through the seemingly infinite range of goods and services available in order to make their own personal selection.

Instead of questioning the users in facilitated groups, the Apple method of designing products involves simply observing them. To do this you need situations in which you can observe what happens when customers discover new products and services. The results are often astounding. Many people behave completely differently from what they themselves had predicted.

Users of digital media are relatively simple to observe using a video camera and a program to record what is happening on the screen. However, watching airline passengers, amateur gardeners or the users of baby buggies is far more complex. Nevertheless, going to the place of use and getting your own impression of the situation always helps in the process of evaluating ideas. Examining theoretical aspects of a product will only give an abstract picture. Thus, the abstract aspects of a product become far too important; for example, the megapixels or gigahertzes, or the

BHP a new car has under its bonnet. To take great photos, an amateur photographer needs more light, not more pixels. And most car drivers will not notice the difference between 120 and 140 BHP, but *will* notice additional leg room or a well-thought-out navigation system.

Observing people is a very old discipline and an anthropologist has a very good chance of getting a job as a Design Thinker.

Quietly and impartially observing exactly what people do with objects and how a product is actually used can provide the basis for developing remarkable and useful products.

ITERATION

If you want to create something new, then get rid of the old stuff. Get rid of the traditional ways of looking at things and doing things. Get rid of the idea you just developed. Even if it hurts. In a world full of ideas, the individual concept is no longer important. Far more important is the process used to find the *right* one. There are tons of ideas floating around. But the creation of innovative products is no longer a linear process; it now involves a team carrying out iterations together, until they reach a new result.

Jonathan Ive, Apple's chief industrial designer, explains that his team are constantly working on new models and visualisations with just one goal: to find faults in the idea and then to create something new, something better.

Apple normally develops features or designs using the 10-3-1 principle. Ten teams start off with ten ideas. This doesn't mean including seven that are just there to make the other three look good, stresses Michael Lopp. On the contrary, all ten teams attempt to present the very best concept they can think up. Various so-called review meetings then take place, attended by all the relevant departments. Design and producibility are both discussed and the three strongest concepts are pursued further. These are then fine tuned and improved upon, sometimes for months on end, until after meetings with senior executives, only the strongest solution is left.

Not every company can afford ten teams in order to develop something. However, the concept works with just a single team drawing up ten ideas, then reducing them to three and finally to just one. And if fewer resources are available, five ideas reduced to three and then to one will also lead to results. The most important thing is to start by thinking up *five* really good solutions. Don't stop after you have had the first two good ideas. It's easy to get overly enthusiastic about your own creativity, and possibly miss the chance of coming up with something much, much better.

Finding the right company structure and staff for this is no easy task. Anyone who wants to get their point across in one of these meetings is going to need a versatile approach: turning problems into solutions means reinventing yourself daily. It's not about coming up with your own brilliant idea, but the iterative process used to draw out the best idea. That's why it's really important that employees are able to review their own ideas with a critical eye.

Modern innovation processes always change an organisation. This is not something to be scared of. In fact, it's important to welcome such change. With the numerous resources available via the Internet, it may feel as if it has never been easier to invent something new. But successfully turning an idea into reality is more difficult, and to do this it is important to always look critically at your own way of working. Ideas on their own are not enough; implementing them is what this is all about.

Agile (or *iterative*) development is the term for the process used by Apple to get ideas working, especially with regard to software. The thinking behind it is that you get better results with a non-bureaucratic, flexible structure. Since conditions are always changing throughout a development process, it is only possible to plan a project roughly. The agile method makes it possible to react flexibly and quickly to new problems and requirements, and to keep modifying the original idea until finally, the best possible product emerges.

On the other hand, when operating in a linear process you can only be as good as those acting before you. In a world of specialists, who can possibly be expected to know everything? Designers? Economists? Technologists? The truth is that no single person is able to fully understand a product like the iPad any more.

Apple puts a lot of effort into solving this problem. It promotes intensive collaboration among the various departments, for example design, technology and production. In this way, it ensures both the innovative nature and the feasibility of the products. The designers meet once a week and think up new ideas without any regard for whether they can be realised or not; it's no problem if they go crazy, says Michael Lopp. Then those same designers attend a weekly meeting with their colleagues from the technical or production departments, and discuss which ideas are feasible and which are not. Even the best idea is worthless if it's not workable.

There is no cheap or simple way to generate great products. This is why high-quality products – not just those from Apple – are not made available online for free. Innovations are, after all, hard work. They stem from a difficult process: one that aims to identify the right concept and then realise it. It is of course important to have competent, experienced staff who are experts in their field. But it's also important that you're willing to invest money. It doesn't matter whether you have these resources in your own firm, or whether you give the job to an outside supplier. Apple, for example, developed the first Macintosh computer with help from external experts. These included Frog Design, an international innovation firm specialising in product design and management consultancy, whose founder, Hartmut Esslinger, claims to have contributed to Apple's success at that time.

Whatever the case may be, you will always need a great team, armed with the means to create something special in a digital world full of possibilities. Forget having a proper development process in place and you can forget the digital future.

In a world full of ideas, the single idea is now of less importance than the process by which the right *one is chosen.*

BUILDING PROTOTYPES

An important component of a successful innovation process is the visualisation of ideas. Apple builds prototypes in the form of mockups that help make design or technical concepts more tangible. They convey not only the product's functionality, but also its spirit. The Apple designers always take great care to ensure that the mockups they create are accurate and realistic. Every pixel has to be just right and there is no dummy text (these are often used to avoid having to write real copy). An Apple prototype looks and feels just like a finished product.

Many companies work with specification sheets and technical concept papers. Apple, however, always develops 'pixel-perfect' prototypes to demonstrate how a product is going to look and function. This helps to focus on the user experience, not just on theoretical aspects such as memory, long battery life and megabytes. Holding and using a product tends to generate *constructive* criticism. On the other hand, if too much is left to the imagination, it may be difficult to see the enormous potential in a particular idea – or to find out what is missing that would make it truly amazing.

Often, people know instinctively that a concept or product is too complex, 'over-loaded' or unsuitable for the intended purpose. Each piece of advice is important, because everyone belongs to the target group – at least as long as they are part of the new ideas meeting. If something is not easy to understand then it just won't make the cut. Successful innovations should not be rocket science, created by a chosen few and only understood by selected users.

Of course, much greater effort is needed to build perfect prototypes. It is far easier just to present sketches or presentations about the product, but putting in the effort is worth it. The persuasive power of an idea is at its greatest when you have a 'finished' and fully functioning product in front of you.

With the help of a prototype, anyone in an organisation can see for themselves whether or not a product is good.

WORKING LIKE A START-UP

Sachin Agarwal, long-time Apple developer, calls for a start-up culture in large corporations. As an experienced Apple insider, he thinks that engineers and designers form Apple's cultural core, with managers who have often previously worked as engineers or designers and therefore understand the daily challenges extremely well. As in a start-up company, the development teams are often very small and focused on specific tasks. The non-negotiable deadline for completion of a project is also regarded as an important basis for the internal 'Apple quality', and resembles the pressure experienced by start-up companies, who have to show their investors at an early stage that their idea can work. A final date of this sort often presents great challenges for the employees; it does, however, help to bring complicated processes to a close and thus increase the pace. At the same time, Agarwal emphasises that Apple places great importance on its employees having enough recreation and recuperation time, and offers them longer than average vacations and excellent health care – which of course sets Apple apart from a typical start-up.

The lack of bureaucracy, the small teams and the loyal employees – often Apple fans before, during, and following their employment – are important factors of success which can all be found in most start-up companies.

Another important aspect of typical start-up culture is the high level of communication skills displayed by the employees. A meeting involving various departments working to a tight deadline, where the participants discuss functions, content, or which refinancing model should be developed, will only be a success if the room is full of good communicators. To ensure a common level of communication, it is important to combine a basic interest in other development fields with a high level of competence in one's own discipline. To set up successful interdisciplinary teams and to give them enough freedom, but also the necessary focus to come up with results, requires different qualifications to those needed in a company with a traditional top-down structure.

People who want to promote innovation, but who have to work within a traditional corporate structure, inevitably long for a fresh culture of this sort. The good news is this: to become as innovative as a start-up company, anyone can start off with their own division, their own department or even with themselves. A small team, made up of people from different departments, with a clearly defined goal and the reassuring feeling that they can concentrate solely on the planned innovations, will produce good results in any company.

Small teams, the ability to make quick decisions, and a clear focus on the goal at hand: development departments that operate like start-ups are faster and more innovative.

BUILDING PLATFORMS

The iPod and the iPhone are now lauded as design classics. However, the design language with which they have been marketed is not the only reason for their success. Just as important is the fact that Apple made these products as part of a whole system consisting of hardware, software and a simple and secure method of purchasing things. With this comprehensive, integrated approach, Apple creates a value chain from the development and production stage right up to the sale of application software. In this way, products become platforms.

A platform serves to link the products to be sold with the processes necessary for this – a complete work of art, which acts as an accessible marketplace for all the market players. It is not the *availability* of a music title on iTunes that can help to make it successful. Far more important is the extremely simple procedure involved in selling or purchasing it.

Many companies regard the web as a new digital sales channel, but have kept their operations much the same as before. An example of this is the production of e-books. Anyone who tries to use a standard format such as ePub to make a textbook available to as many devices as possible but develops it in the traditional way, first producing the printed book and then 'digitalising' it, is still thinking within conventional structures. A textbook, often full of illustrations, graphics and other elements of design, has to be digitally reinvented from cover to cover. A whole new process is necessary, because the real potential lies in the digitalisation of the *entire* value chain.

If you want to transform products and services for the digital world, the platform concept is of enormous importance.

Companies have to modernise the often outdated structure of their traditional value chains if they want to be successful players in the market of the future.

Because no standard software for playing digital music was available, Apple bought an MP3 playback program called SoundJam and enhanced it to create the iTunes Music Store. The decision to offer everything from a single source was not a purely strategic one, but was taken largely out of necessity, as there was no adequate technology available with which Apple could successfully position its devices. In developing a complete system of its own, Apple did not reinvent music, but it did create a brand new value chain, and in 2007 it received a Grammy for its efforts.

Other successful firms have also developed platforms. Facebook, for example, realised early on that a developer platform could encourage growth in the market for social networks. A technical interface allows developers to offer their own programs on the Facebook website. The resulting universe of programs and services played an important part in making the company market leader in the social network field.

By developing a system that would simplify the distribution of applications for mobile phones, Apple laid the foundations for the commercial success of the iPhone. It created an Internet shop, the app store, where you can choose from hundreds of thousands of programs for smartphones, almost all of them created by developers who do not work for Apple. At the same time, Apple extended the value chain to include not only the purchase of applications on the Internet, but also the development of the apps themselves. To make sure that as many programs as possible are available for the iPhone and its sister devices, Apple provides a tool with which software can be developed. The developers get 70 per cent of the proceeds and Apple takes 30 per cent for billing and processing the transaction.

The development of the iPhone therefore involved the creation of not just a telephone, but also a complete platform, and to do this

Apple had to rethink the value chain. This approach can also be valuable in other industries and sectors. If the suppliers are unable to deliver a particular component then it may be worth considering producing it yourself until a new supplier is found.

An ideal platform integrates all the aspects of the product benefit into a simple customer-centric system.

COMMUNICATION

DESIGNING

Apple products are successful because, among other things, they have their own characteristic design. Apple is among the few firms that have made unique industrial design part of their philosophy right from the start. Since the 1984 launch of the Macintosh – the first commercial computer with a mouse, a graphical user interface and a PC integrated into the monitor – Apple has been known for excellent design.

With numerous permanent exhibits in the Museum of Modern Art in New York, countless awards and its constantly grow-ing success, Apple has shown that design can be one of the decisive success factors for a company.

In the last century no applied art discipline was so dominated by Europeans as design. Jonathan Ive often cites Dieter Rams as one of his inspirations. Together with his contemporaries Artur and Erwin Braun, Rams led the revolutionary industrial design movement in the 1950s and 1960s. He invented numerous household items for the German company Braun, and his work is also included in the permanent exhibition in the Museum of Modern Art. His creations are timeless and functional and have their own special identity.

Rams therefore did the groundwork and Jonathan Ive enhanced it for the new century. If you look at Braun's pocket calculators, stereo hi-fi systems and movie cameras, dating from decades back but with timeless appeal, you cannot but be reminded of current Apple products. Borrowing from earlier designers has helped make the Apple products as successful as they are.

Dieter Rams identified ten principles of

'good design', which are still as relevant today as they were forty years ago:

- *Good design is innovative*
- *Good design makes a product useful*
- *Good design is aesthetic*
- *Good design makes a product understandable*
- *Good design is honest*
- *Good design is unobtrusive*
- *Good design is long-lasting*
- *Good design is thorough down to the last detail*
- *Good design is environmentally friendly*
- *Good design is as little design as possible*

People who design products do not always work for a premium brand like Braun or Apple. In fact, in certain sectors highly influenced by trends, longevity can sometimes be a drawback. However, even those who can't or don't want to follow all these rules have to admit that Apple has had remarkable success with its own interpretation of them, even (and indeed especially) in the mass market.

In contrast to the 1950s and 1960s, when the design behind certain trends was seen as merely an adjunct, good timeless design has now itself become a trend. Great design does not just make a product unmistakable; it also demonstrates the owner's individuality. Status symbols such as high-end car brands and handbags are almost always based on a distinctive design.

With the exception of sectors that are obviously design driven, such as the fashion industry, design is still regarded by many companies as an unnecessary frill. It is, however, similar to communication: you cannot avoid it. The way a product looks plays an important role in the purchase decision, so every company should think about the design at as early a stage as possible.

Apple, as a brand, stands for consistently formal design that is recognisable throughout the product categories. Anyone looking for inspiration when designing a product would be well advised to take a look at a few Apple devices in an Apple store or design museum.

Investing time in good design for a specific product is the best way to show the world that it is unique.

BELIEVING

The release of a new Apple product just wouldn't be the same without the rumours that precede it. These are either spread deliberately, or are an effective by-product of Apple's normally secretive communication strategy. Whatever the reason may be for the thousands of articles that appear in blogs and magazines, in which self-appointed insiders announce that they have found out something about the new product, it works! You will seldom find a company surrounded by so many legends as the firm from Cupertino.

There are bloggers who will travel to the Far East in an attempt to find out something new from the suppliers. Others analyse every detail of Apple's patent applications. Patent sketches, which often look like children's drawings, provide information about new strategies. Some fans have even created perfect photomontages, apparently showing the new product, and which sometimes even make it into the mass media. Even though Apple employees risk being fired if they reveal anything, information is consistently leaked. People *love* rumours about new Apple products and just can't wait for the official announcements – the legendary Keynotes. But why is this?

Marketing consultant and bestselling author Simon Sinek tells us: 'People don't buy what you do – they buy what you believe.' Apple's marketing strategy focuses on transforming technical functions into needs.

When Steve Jobs returned to Apple in 1997, he had the stirring commercial 'Think Different' made, featuring famous personalities such as Picasso and Maria Callas. This reflects Simon Sinek's philosophy: it is a homage to all those who think differently, and still forms the basis of Apple's brand identity. Low market share at the end of the 1990s meant that an image had to be created that showed loyal fans they were right in their decision to buy computers from the underdog Apple instead of PCs. The commercial and the image it helped create led millions of people to decide that this was a company they believed in. And by buying Apple products, they were able to show that they too were different.

Apple uses emotions to sell products. Its employees consistently state that Apple is, quite simply, *different*. The company is essentially the complete opposite of all the other computer and consumer electronics manufacturers. Although Apple has become a more dominant player in the last decade and many of its products have entered the mainstream, owners of an iPhone or iPad often still have the feeling that they are somehow different from other consumers, or at least that they belong to a special community.

The two most important marketing campaigns of recent years reveal how Apple nurtures its image of being different and makes people want to be part of the Apple community.

The 'Switch' campaign was launched in 2002 and showed people – some of them famous – explaining in a very personal way why they had switched to Apple. The focus was not on device functions, but rather on personal and sometimes emotional reasons for switching to Apple. The cellist Yo-Yo Ma, for example, explained that he is 'technically challenged', and that's why he loves something as simple and beautiful as an Apple computer.

The award-winning 'Get a Mac' campaign also focused on people and their needs; in fact, not a single product was shown. Everyone remembers the laid-back young guy and the stuffy suit wearer, who respectively represent the Mac and the PC; of course, the Mac always has the best solution to the issues that many Windows users experience daily. In sixty seconds the two of them have a discussion about the problems the uptight guy has with his Windows machine and the solutions that the relaxed one can provide with his Mac.

Apple is also uniquely strong in the consistency with which it implements its corporate design across all aspects of the brand. The perfection and sophistication of the products are clearly reflected in all corporate communication. The minimalist design of the commercials, the product photos and the furnishing of the Apple stores is all so perfectly coordinated that no one could ever mistake the brand behind it.

People do not buy an Apple product because of its design or its functions but because Apple believes in something in which they also want to believe.

PUTTING THE PRODUCT
IN THE SPOTLIGHT

If there's one company that knows how to put its products in the spotlight, it's Apple. Imitation is the sincerest form of flattery, and this area of its expertise is the one that people most commonly try to copy. Many companies model the way they present their products on Apple. Web designers try to reproduce its minimalist website. And Apple's simple strategies regarding product photographs and communication are also much emulated. It is not without reason that a new visual concept from Apple usually becomes a trendsetter and the inspiration for advertising campaigns for products as diverse as automobiles and sports shoes.

So what are the main characteristics of Apple's advertising, and what makes it so successful? Let's look at the example of the light and extremely compact MacBook Air. In one television commercial the ultra-thin device is shown being taken out of an envelope, to demonstrate just how thin it really is. The principal benefit of the product is demonstrated using a clear and instantly comprehensible image.

The famous iPod 'silhouette' commercials with their vivid colours and white headphones convey the message: listening to music on an iPod is fun! The black silhouettes were an ideal projection screen for anyone who wanted to see themselves in that commercial. Instead of dealing with gigabytes or other technical features, it conveyed a message that was simply about the personal pleasure that could be derived from listening to music.

The iPod Touch is positioned as a device that allows you to communicate by video. The print ads and TV commercials show families, couples and grandparents who can speak to and see each other using the FaceTime video chat feature. As we have seen with other products, the iPod Touch is not positioned by gigabytes, screen resolution or other technical features but by one clear message.

It is always a specific user need that takes centre stage in the advertising and makes it special. It would be wrong to think in terms of interfaces, synergies and usability etc., because the product has to be backed up by a specific and very evident benefit. Buzzwords alone are rarely helpful. If you cannot name a clear product advantage, then there probably isn't one and you'll have to think carefully about how to make the product a success. When positioning a product, a marketing department or advertising agency can only be as good as the product idea itself.

Many a good product has been discussed to death: that's why advertising has to be based on just a few key benefits. Products developed by Apple for professional users, such as the

Final Cut Pro video-editing software, offer literally hundreds of functions and options. On the web, however, Apple focuses on just a few important features and banishes the rest to the list of technical details.

Anyone who wants to know whether their product is actually good and whether people will understand it should attempt to put together a clear and accessible presentation. Creating slides with single words and no long lists means being clearly focused and reducing things down to the essentials. The resulting presentation will serve as a better briefing for employees and suppliers than a twelve-page document containing everything – and nothing.

Apple showcases its products with an emphasis not on technical details but rather on customer benefits.

SENDING A CLEAR
MESSAGE

One enormous advantage of the Internet is the high level of transparency it creates for the consumer, especially regarding reviews of products and services. The Internet brings customers together. They can search for the names of products, or scan the bar code of an item, and immediately access all the important information and any reviews that have been written.

If a product and its advantages have to be explained at length, no one in a department store is going to take the time to find out whether their choice is the right one. The digital success of a product is therefore highly dependent on whether the product benefits can be described in a single simple sentence. It's not just the availability of information that's important. Digitally minded people who use Facebook or other social media platforms receive a vast number of recommendations, and news of great products that are easy to explain spreads like wildfire. People tend to talk about products with an obvious benefit as if they were exciting news headlines you just *have* to tell your friends about.

Finding the one compelling selling point of a complicated product should not be left to the marketing or PR department. A crucial characteristic should always be an important part of the product development process.

Products and services should be examined early on regarding their suitability for the digital era. Can your product survive in a transparent world? In the past, products were protected from too much harsh criticism by the lack of transparency. Today it's quite normal to let everyone know what you think about them. Brands and products are dragged into the public arena and discussed openly.

Does everyone in a company really know why their product is special? What single sentence could you use to describe the product – not the official line, but the real reason why a customer would buy it? Without this reason, no product will be able to survive the digital revolution. Too many companies spend their time putting together PowerPoint presentations, with long lists showing the various advantages of each product. An overdose of text and graphics serves to hide the fact that there is no simple reason to buy the product. If a product manager cannot list the advantages of his product on a single slide then it is probably going to be difficult to reach any significant market share.

Coming up with the best ideas in an iterative process that involves intense communication with colleagues will always require a clear vision. That's why creating 'a great app' is not really the best starting point for a successful campaign.

When the first iPad slogan ('A magical and revolutionary device at an unbelievable price') was made public, many people were surprised at the use of the word 'magical'. Yes, it *is* revolutionary, and we can talk about the price, but 'magical'? Many regarded the iPad as superfluous because of its lack of particular features, but after a couple of months people were saying that you shouldn't criticise the iPad until you've spent twenty-four hours with it and that you will only realise its true benefits when you use it. And that's what they meant by 'magical'. It doesn't matter whether Apple really did have this sentence in mind when they started the development process, or whether it evolved over a whole series of meetings. More important is that it describes the device *and* the user experience in a concise and attractive way.

A clear message, preferably one that describes the product in just one sentence, creates clarity regarding both the product and one's own mindset.

SUPPORTING INDIVIDUALITY

Apple's products send a clear message: what you see here are beautiful, desirable objects that can perform a certain task extremely well. The focus is on the product experience whereas the technical details take a back seat. The Apple brand still has a hint of rebellion to it, and despite the fact that it is now very much in the mainstream most customers still regard it as something special.

Apple only offers a very limited number of products – a strategy that appears to disregard the individuality of its customers. Other producers seem to offer an individual product for almost every niche and are thus able to sell more smartphones than Apple. So is it really true that Apple is failing to meet people's individual needs with its limited product range?

The answer is no, because Apple appeals to the individuality of its customers not by offering a wide range of hardware options, but with software and marketplaces, such as iTunes and the app store, that are easy to navigate. One example: someone who puts together his own individual computer in a specialist shop will (usually) get exactly what he ordered. But the options selected are often influenced by price and numerous technical specifications, which are so complicated that only those who count computer assembly as a hobby can really benefit. The vast majority of consumers are therefore looking for a ready-made, fully functioning solution created for them by innovative developers.

The individuality of most customers today is only reflected in how they *use* the PC. This is where Apple can take advantage of its enormous expertise in developing simple systems that anyone can use. The technology takes a secondary role and the system is determined by the required application. Most people are able to use a Mac to express their own creativity and individuality. And to this end, Apple has designed a whole range of software.

With iPhoto, you can organise and edit your photos, create slideshows and share images with others. You can also use the software to design and order a photo album with your own photos. The program is easy to use, requiring no specialist knowledge. With Garageband, people without any musical background can create music, record it, and then burn it to CD or share it online. Pages is Apple's answer to Word. Using the templates and other options, even beginners can produce flyers, brochures and invitations. And with iMovie, Apple has provided amateur filmmakers with a tool to edit and share films that is powerful in its simplicity. Apple has invested millions to tie in these and other programs to its operating system and hardware. The underlying message is: with Apple products, you can express yourself in a creative and individual way.

Then there's the iPhone. Before the iPhone, manufacturers decided what programs their phones were equipped with. Ever since the dawn of the app store, customers can use apps to adapt their phones to their individual needs. Anyone interested in astronomy can find a whole range of apps to suit their requirements; the same applies for the manager who travels a lot and relies on the latest travel information.

Artists use painting apps to create completely new works of art, sometimes collaborating with colleagues from around the world. DJs use special apps to lay down tunes, employing a number of networked iPads to create a completely new music experience. With hundreds of thousands of apps the individual needs of nearly every customer are met. In fact, precisely because of its standardisation of products and platforms, Apple is able to ensure maximum customisability for the user. For developers it is far easier to produce things for a small range of products than for heterogenic and diverse hardware.

Many app developers have had this painful experience when attempting to adapt a successful iOS app – the operating system for mobile devices from Apple – for other platforms such as Android. The cost of supporting the multiple screen sizes and options offered by the respective hardware often exceeds the budget and expected profits from a field where sales are much lower anyway. It is only when developers really throw themselves into the task that a brilliant app can be created, which in turn can help customer groups enjoy greater individuality.

Motivating freelance designers to produce content for your own standardised marketplace means you can also satisfy all types of niche needs in the most diverse customer groups.

INITIAL
CONCLUSIONS

For over thirty years, Apple has been inspiring people. What started as an idea to create useful, accessible products for everyone has now turned into the world's most valuable company.

The first section of this book describes how Apple operates and what makes the company unique. These concepts provide a framework for one's own personal ideas: a collection of thoughts and inspirations that can help you develop your own products and services. The key aspects include a unique mindset, a radical development model, and Apple's world-famous communication strategy.

MINDSET

Apple's mindset can be compared with that of a mid-sized company. Whether it's a mail-order business, or a company selling cars, groceries, furniture or machines, with a pragmatic approach and common sense, the founders of many mid-sized companies have laid the foundations for their success. But the ability to say no and the decision to offer less than one's competitors is also very much part of this tradition. Many devices from Braun, for example, had fewer functions than those sold by competitor companies – the basis for the remarkably 'clean' design.

Unfortunately, offering less and saying no is never enough. In an age of free global markets, it is essential to control your market and products to survive. Just as coffee machine companies attempt to sell their capsules exclusively for as long as possible and keep the competition at bay, while digital booksellers try to tie in their customers to their own technical universe, so too, when it comes to your own products, you must ask the question: how can I ensure that my customers stay with me and pay me for my efforts? Customers do, however, accept closed, tightly controlled systems if they are particularly user friendly and help to solve a real problem, as demonstrated by Apple.

In the end, Apple is the best example of what still holds true: a company has to invent its own products. If customers are to become fans, always eager to own the latest version of a product, then the invention must come from the inventor. In contrast, products that have been developed using crowdsourcing will never be anything more than average.

PRODUCT DEVELOPMENT

To generate unique inventions, you need to have in place processes and methods that bring together a team of specialists and inspire them to deliver excellence. With Design Thinking, it was not only Apple that revolutionised its development process, but so did many other companies. The basic idea is pretty simple: if specialists from various fields are to work together in a more creative way, then they have to work as a designer does. Creating and destroying, trial and error, testing and improving. This is the only way to narrow down the endless possibilities and get the show on the road.

Thinking like a designer doesn't mean that you actually have to be one or that you will automatically become one. It is, however, an essential tool for a start-up culture that can help to move things forward, particularly in the digital age. In large, traditional companies in particular, this is a very effective way to speed up the innovation process.

Many successful digital products are platforms: networked systems where market participants can make contact with each other. Music lovers and music labels, app developers and iPhone users, film producers and cineastes, book lovers and publishers. Digital platforms are, however, more than just a marketplace; they represent the digital version of what used to be an analogue value chain. The more integrated and interwoven the individual steps, the more convincing the platform product.

COMMUNICATION

As with every other company Apple needs to sell its products, so it has to communicate. Here, the product design plays a leading role. A key component of the communication strategy is simply to design beautiful, classy, desirable products. The advertising task is then remarkably simple: just focus on the essentials, in other words the product photo and just one or two sentences that make it absolutely clear why the product is so special from the perspective of the customer. In addition, Apple sells a particular attitude to life – a feeling of being somehow different – and has thus become a projection screen for the customer. With its concept of motivating freelance developers to use its platforms to develop things, Apple has also discovered a unique way of supporting the individuality of its customers without having to develop specific products for every niche.

A DIFFERENCE YOU CAN FEEL

In what way can Apple's approach help to develop digital products? And how can you learn from Apple – no matter how big or small your business?

The basic insight is that the future of digital products can be seen in just one clear, comprehensible message. This message answers the question: what tangible difference sets the product apart from its competitors? In a world full of opportunities, offers and products, success depends more than ever on whether customers, with their limited attention spans, can feel what a product is all about. Only when the 'fast' part of the brain, which guides us most of the time, gives us the go-ahead, can the slower, rational part of the brain allow us to embrace an idea. Everything else – anything that fails to catch the attention of the fast part of the brain – is blocked out as a form of self-protection and has no effect at all.

In his book *Thinking, Fast and Slow,* Daniel Kahneman explains that the decisions and actions we take are controlled by a sort of autopilot inside us. This even applies to the academic elite. If, in a world full of distractions, you want to sell something, it is essential to address the consumer's fast-thinking, instinctive side first. Whether a product has a large number of technical features or not is only important at a later stage once the customer is already on autopilot. Only then do technical benefits and product details come into play. First of all it is important that you *feel* something.

It's no longer just advertising that 'emotionalises' a product. A good TV commercial may be able to sell special products in the moment and in the next few years, but changes in media use, the transparency available via the Net and a growing aversion in customers to advertising will increasingly mean that the product has to be its own commercial. It needs to quickly tell the customer why it shouldn't be ignored, and why it's worth having a second look at. This especially applies to digital products such as online shops and apps.

This is the sort of product that Apple creates. An iPod does not just have a beautiful clean design for the sake of it. It has the advantage of being able to send its message directly to the customer: the message that it is different and well worth looking at more closely. This insight represents an enormous opportunity not just for Apple. Perhaps the company is so successful because the world has become so fast-moving and complex. The products bearing the bitten apple logo really do stand out from the crowd. You can *feel* the difference.

Apple develops products that are self-explanatory when it comes to communicating their benefits. The company is in a unique position in the market and most competitors don't seem to realise this.

In the second section of this book, the concepts explored in the first section will be applied to imaginary scenarios. This is not so much about any real implementation, or the feasibility of the products and concepts described, but more about experimental ideas for markets in which Apple is not (yet) present.

WHAT WOULD
APPLE DO?

AN APPLE CAR

When developers create new cars, they do so in a market characterised by a constant pressure to innovate. The media is full of prototypes of innovative automobiles and they even appear in big Hollywood movies. And since fears about climate change have become a widespread concern, work has begun on concept cars that promise to combine low fuel consumption with top performance. Yet despite high demands on individual mobility, you will seldom find a car that is significantly different to the others.

WHAT WOULD APPLE DO TO CREATE A
COMPLETELY NEW TYPE OF CAR?

What would make people more willing to buy a car that is different from anything they've ever seen? This is often where researchers come in. They ask questions such as 'What does today's consumer want?', and studies are undertaken to find the answer. Experts are consulted, target group profiles are compiled and scientific principles are applied to determine the most important features of the new car. Studies are analysed for months or years on end, and ideas are then evaluated based on the findings.

But even without complex analyses, our common sense tells us that the increasing number of practically interchangeable cars is in stark contrast to a world striving for more individuality. Finding a solution to this problem is not only a formidable challenge; it could also be a source of enormous potential. So it's time to start observing car drivers and watching what they do – preferably with no preconceptions – to find out what they *really* want. In their choice of car, people say something about themselves. Perhaps they want to demonstrate good taste and individuality, or express themselves by customising the vehicle and its appearance. Others will decorate their cars with stickers or other items. There is also an enormous market for auto tuning, allowing customers to have their own individual technical and visual details added to their vehicles.

How would you define the new car, so that everyone would immediately understand where you're coming from – the sort of description that could be the starting point for the development process? The environmentally friendliest automobile? The most flexible one? The first car that can sense dangerous situations? Or, in the case of *our* new invention, the most highly personalised car? The description chosen is the answer to the question 'Why should the customer buy this new car?' At the same time, it also forms the marketing and communication strategy. It's never a good idea to let the marketing department get on with the job on their own – marketing the new car by deciding which features have a good ring to them and then advertising them with the same old platitudes and so-called added emotion.

The production of 'off the rack' cars is already highly complex, so if we want to put individuality in the spotlight, things are going to get even more complex for everyone involved. Now is the time to decide which business model could help the new product conquer the market. Is, for example, a business model in which the energy giants earn enormous profits from petrol really a status quo that can't be challenged? Or can we learn from the manufacturers of printers and coffee machines and adapt the ink cartridge system for producing and selling cars, to build a platform that offers more than just the car as a product? Nothing has to stay the same. So why can't a car giant such as Ford buy an energy company or a chain of petrol stations and use them for Ford automobiles? All the prices could be newly calculated, from the selling price of the car to the litre price for the petrol, because by expanding the business model, all services such as repairs and maintenance and also the energy used would come from Ford. This would provide the company with a wider source of income and the chance to earn money throughout the car's life cycle. Perhaps in the long term, cross-subsidising the selling price of an individualised automobile will make an environmental performance possible that just can't be achieved if you get bogged down in the usual business models.

Today's cars are built by automobile manufacturers and their parts suppliers. A complex value chain that is in constant battle with a whole range of formats and systems. Despite many attempts to standardise and harmonise things, a single 'operating system' for cars remains a dream. One way forward could be to define an operating system for building automobiles that involves the active participation of all parties. This would lead to a decrease in development and production costs that would in turn mean that more variety and more options could be made available to the customer. We're talking about strict modular construction as part of a simple but flexible technical system. Thanks to the interfaces being made available, even the smallest of firms will be able to manufacture highly specialised components that customers can use in the simplest possible way – in other words, plug and play.

Essentially, customers visit an automobile 'department store', purchase fully compatible components together with an engine and assemble their own individual dream car themselves. Like Apple's apps, the components come from a variety of developers, but also from the car manufacturer itself. In principle, a company like Volkswagen could open up existing efforts to establish identical development technologies for several brands and let a wide developer community take part.

The new car's design will have to clearly reflect its high level of individuality, simple handling and efficiency. To do this, we will have to do away with the traditional components in its basic structure, perhaps by integrating a new kind of motor into the wheels, which means many of the components of today's cars would no longer be needed. The wheels containing the motor would be coordinated with each other using an internal communication system, so numerous new ways of designing the bodywork would be possible. Perhaps a super-slim automobile in which four people can sit one behind the other, or a one-seater for driving locally – the list goes on and on.

At the end of this process, we see not just a modern car, but a completely new platform for producing individualised vehicles which are put together by the customers themselves using components from numerous developers.

Employing a technical 'operating system' that standardises the components of a car enables small companies to offer modular components. The customer is thus able to put together his or her own personal vehicle.

A KITCHEN BY APPLE

People are prepared to spend a great deal of money on a fitted kitchen. The market for kitchens and kitchen appliances is huge, but the business is also extremely traditional. Automobile companies, for example, have long been using new digital technology to set themselves apart from their competitors, whereas time seems to have stood still in the kitchen sector. Apart from a few niche companies, it is hard to find any truly innovative kitchen solutions. However, this is an area with enormous potential.

WHAT WOULD APPLE DO TO CREATE AN
INNOVATIVE KITCHEN?

The Apple kitchen will be simple but beautiful, because great care has been taken to reduce the many possibilities to the necessary minimum and keep saying no. Putting it together will be an enjoyable experience. The surfaces and materials are high quality and ecologically sustainable. All the components are standardised and easy to operate, and you don't need to read loads of manuals before you can get cooking in your new kitchen. Quite the contrary.

The whole kitchen is an interlinked digital system. The user who wants to cook a particular recipe downloads it from the computer, which is connected to all the kitchen appliances, using its own database or the Internet. The kitchen then leads the user step by step through the program. The digital recipe works like an app that programs the various system components: the cooker, the fridge, the cupboards and the microwave. Each appliance is controlled by a touchscreen large enough to show videos. In this way, the cook is shown how to fillet a fish and the oven displays the time remaining until the vegetables are ready. Acoustic signals help you keep track of everything. Every step is demonstrated in a video at precisely the right moment. The oven automatically heats up to the required temperature, which is then regulated during cooking. In the small individual freezing compartments, the food for the recipe is defrosted right on time. This is all possible because the kitchen 'knows' where the ingredients for the recipe are kept. The drawers and containers are coded and can thus be digitally accessed. In this way, our new kitchen can not only locate all the ingredients for a particular recipe, but can order them as well if necessary.

The intelligent kitchen uses its data to suggest recipes incorporating the food available, always giving priority to products that have almost reached the end of their shelf life. To allow for easy programming of recipes, an infrastructure is employed that reminds us of the development and sale of apps. Cookery book authors can use a simple authoring tool to create recipes for the new kitchen and sell them. The individual cooking steps can be displayed in a variety of ways, with videos showing you what to do, step by step; these can be humorous, down to earth, or even unconventional and quirky.

The kitchen can determine purchase frequencies based on the occupant's habits and suggests shopping lists according to the space available and the number of family members currently at home. Our new kitchen is not just a product; it also serves as a platform.

Today, manufacturers of kitchens earn their money by selling kitchen furniture and electrical appliances. Our new kitchen, however, comes with a nationwide customer service organisation that sells, assembles and services it. The added bonus is that the customer service department also has a grocery delivery service and deals with everything from supplying the food to picking up the empties. The customer can relax in the knowledge that everything is being taken care of. To provide this comprehensive service, it will be necessary to work closely with established companies in the food sector and tie them into the whole concept.

Individual appliances communicate with other digital appliances within their own network and can thus automatically download the latest drivers and configurations. Using the Internet, the kitchen regularly provides information, for example about the average energy consumption of other kitchens, and warns its users if one of the appliances is using too much energy.

Apple will, however, probably not bother building robots that can cook, preferring instead to put its faith in the age-old traditions and the passion involved in cooking. This is one thing the people should do themselves.

A kitchen gets networked. All the appliances have a common interface and are connected to a central customer service department that not only provides technical service, but also delivers groceries direct to the doorstep. Recipes – in the form of apps – control the entire infrastructure of the kitchen.

AN APPLE TV

For years, specialists have been talking about media convergence: the merging of media such as television, radio and Internet. However, millions of people still sit in front of their television sets every day just zapping through the channels and recording films. Although Apple is already trying to enter this market with a set-top box, the big question still remains.

WHAT WOULD APPLE DO TO BUILD AN INNOVATIVE TELEVISION SET?

A good starting point is to ask ourselves what we personally dislike about the televisions available today. The remote controls are too complicated; there is never anything good on TV; and the commercials are annoying – these are the sort of comments that just about everyone has heard at least once. And there are countless magazines that tell amateur technicians about all the things you can do with the various devices. Television is a science of cables, gadgets and remote controls. For some people it's a hobby similar to computer assembly, but for most it's just a nuisance.

A television set is not just for playing films or watching live broadcasts; it is also a piece of furniture, which normally has a prominent place in the room. It is a status symbol, and it would seem that the more options it has to offer the better. However, these options often just confuse people and it takes time to understand everything. Just to watch a football game you often have to work with up to five different appliances. In fact, it would be really good if someone started saying no.

Apple will therefore rely on the common sense of its developers and decide that a television set must be easy to use, without an overwhelming number of accessories and a pile of cables. The many additional gadgets and the technical jargon used by salespeople are far too complicated. Only the important functions should be included when developing the new product. The user wants to buy the appliance, take it home, and simply turn it on to start watching TV.

Similar to the iMac, the new Apple television set is flat and has all the necessary devices integrated into its housing. The technology disappears behind the design but is nevertheless really special; the television set consists of a screen and a computer. The user only needs one device to watch TV, surf the web and play rented films or music. What is missing is a traditional receiver with, for example, satellite or cable; this is because everything you watch on this new TV is supplied to your living room by the Internet.

If this television is going to earn money in a fiercely competitive market, it has to offer something really new: a new technical platform for all the different market players – just like the iPod and the iPhone. Thus, the supplier thus not only earns money by selling the appliance, but also through a new TV app store.

Our new television set is more than just a product: it's a platform for TV apps. The user can play games as if he or she were using a console and communicate via the Internet. Facebook and Google have new TV apps, as do the local newspaper and the sports channel. Various suppliers compete for the best digital video recorder program, and TV stations show advertising via split screen during the shows. Game shows allow the viewers to interact using their new television, and talk shows can switch to viewers' living rooms and ask them questions. Like the iPad today, the television just needs the right app to transform itself into a brand new device. Sometimes it's a game console, sometimes a video conference system and at other times simply a traditional movie player. There's one app per TV station and sometimes for special events, such as the final game in a world championship sports event, there's an app for a particular broadcast.

The innovative television set will also provide the advertising industry with new ways of making brands more tangible, for example by introducing interactive commercials. If you want to advertise a vacuum cleaner just before an evening TV show, you can book an app that appears in the corner of the screen following your commercial. If the viewer wants more information about the product and clicks on the app, the program puts the show on hold until the viewer is ready. During films and shows, free apps are shown that the user can 'collect' and view later at his leisure. The traditional commercial can take on a completely new dimension with this television set, because it provides an interactive experience, during primetime television hours.

Thanks to the new television, the trend towards individualised viewing will increase even further, broadening the scope for the advertising industry to get to work. Hiring films is expensive, and few people are prepared to pay every evening for the movies they watch. The new television set will allow advertisers to present whole packages of shows for free and in return enjoy the undivided attention of the viewer. If, however, the viewer is planning a guys' night and wants to watch the complete *Matrix* trilogy without being interrupted by commercials, he can pay to hire it from the digital video library. Or he can access a 'guys' night' show package sponsored by a car manufacturer for free. The advertisers know the program environment, because they pick the films themselves and are thus able to communicate in a variety of creative ways. They can present movies that transport their individual messages well and use short films that fit perfectly to the main feature instead of commercials. TV stations will produce series just as they do today, and show them for free, sponsored by advertisers.

The time and effort needed to develop a TV platform of this kind will dissuade most manufacturers from taking this path. Not only Google and Apple, but also companies like Sony, already have devices on the market that you can plug into your television set. The problem is, however, that none of these offers a comprehensive platform. They also fail to address the problem of numerous cables and attachments: there is no single unit that can do everything. And most importantly, the products currently on offer do not incorporate modern marketplaces where developers have the chance to offer their own applications. Nevertheless, the television set of the future has the potential to become a billion-dollar market.

By connecting television to a TV app store, the successful concepts associated with the Apple app store can be enhanced and expanded even further – this time right in the living room.

AN E-LEARNING PLATFORM FROM APPLE

Education and lifelong learning are key social issues. But despite this, schools, universities and other places of education rarely support the learning process by utilising new media to its full potential. Although many e-learning projects exist, there is still no general solution in sight that would be of any real benefit to the modern teacher. Even though it's not only students, but also suppliers and developers of educational software, who would benefit from an innovative digital marketplace for educational offers, traditional mindsets and antiquated ways of doing things still stand in the way of any comprehensive digitalisation.

WHAT WOULD APPLE DO TO DEVELOP AN INNOVATIVE E-LEARNING PLATFORM?

Anyone studying at high school, university or indeed at home needs to manage his or her time effectively. Many people want to learn new things to advance their careers. The chances of promotion or just being able to manage a job better will increase when you have the relevant professional qualifications. Companies also often offer their employees advanced training courses, many of which are externally sourced and involve honing professional skills such as negotiation techniques for salesmen, holding presentations and using Microsoft Office. Today, company employees, freelancers and other interested parties need someone who can not only teach the subject matter effectively, but also offer additional flexible solutions that reflect their own (digital) reality.

Those who teach, for example freelance

trainers, universities and colleges, schools and in-house training departments, are usually able to prepare and convey knowledge in a didactically sound way. Some offers are highly specialised and of interest to only a few people. On the other hand, some offers are much sought after, for example basic qualifications in MS Office software, management or website development.

The key element of an e-learning platform is the networking that takes place between teachers and those wanting to learn. Through this platform everyone can meet up virtually and exchange information. It's a combination of search engine, app store and a community like Facebook, and all the learning units can be uploaded here. Extremely productive students or those with time on their hands can read the material in advance if they so wish. Less talented students, on the other hand, have more time to work through the lessons.

The e-learning platform works like an online network. The students are in constant contact with the other members. Where they actually are is not important; learning could take place at home, in an Internet café or in the company. All they need is a computer and access to the web. Nevertheless, a face-to-face meeting is occasionally necessary in order to exchange information, present ideas and get to know each other. As all participants use laptops and tablets on which all the information and programs are installed, they can meet with the other students in online conferences and with the tutors for group work. The web portal can also be used by textbook publishers, coaching academies, providers of further education and other suppliers to upload learning units that are available, following approval by a central authority, into the learning app pool.

A learning app incorporates the texts, images and videos that are needed for a particular subject, and also the tools for studying and evaluating what has been learned. The results can be shared on the platform, thus allowing a student to compare his or her own progress with that of others. When a student has to prepare a project or a report, this can be done using the platform. In this way the findings and results of their work are returned to the pool so that others can benefit from them.

An app must be thematically and didactically sound, so all the apps are subject to a regularly updated quality check. This quality assurance is carried out both by the supplier of the e-learning platform and by the involved parties themselves. Anyone who has worked through a learning unit and noticed that it doesn't work properly can leave a comment in the app store, and thus help to ensure that the developer makes the necessary corrections. Students with a certain amount of technical skill can compile their own learning units and thus ensure that the content remains up to date, while also making money. A special authoring program allows anyone, whether students or teachers, to create their own learning app. This concept can already be seen at work today: with iBooks Author, Apple has created an authoring application for textbooks which allows anyone to process what they have learned and also to test themselves using the contents of the book.

Not only will the obvious suppliers such as publishers of schoolbooks be active in the app store, but independent developers will also be able to upload their own apps, subject to approval. By including this highly dynamic type of business, the willingness to innovate will increase and a whole new market will be created.

If, for example, a hypothetical learning unit called 'digital marketing' from the user's own university gets a lot of bad reviews, the student can download the corresponding lesson from another university. He can illustrate the differences and show his tutors where the weaknesses are. Anyone who doesn't want to start a university course, but wants to learn new skills alongside his job, has access to all the learning units in the marketplace. Although an unofficial student will have to pay more for the units, the users can rest assured that they will benefit from the highest quality of teaching and knowledge imparted.

Providing locations where students and teachers can also meet, such as lecture theatres, classrooms and meeting rooms in companies, remains an important task that must be accomplished outside the e-learning platform. Because education cannot be reduced to reading books and working through learning apps alone, it must continue to include discussions and activities where the participant is physically present.

No matter who really does get to run a platform of this kind – it could be a private company or a state institution – it will, as the first comprehensive platform for education, offer the parties involved completely new ways of earning money in the digital world.

The business model is an app store with learning units: using a simple authoring tool, students can develop and sell their own learning apps.

AN APPLE TRAVEL AGENT

Travel is one of the world's largest industries. People are travelling more than ever before, and many prefer to book their journey on the Internet. There are numerous portals and providers, most of which look pretty much the same. This is a supply-driven market that is coming under increasing price pressure in the middle and lower price segments. The customer experience is often characterised by nebulous travel regulations and the fear that the most important time of the year might turn into a disaster.

WHAT WOULD APPLE DO TO REVOLUTION-
ISE THE TRAVEL INDUSTRY?

We have almost all experienced the problems of booking a holiday or business trip on the Internet. This can involve no end of booking templates, emails and incorrect data, followed by an inexplicably long wait just to have the availability confirmed.

Let's assume that the destination is a big town. You have to book a cheap flight, and then a hotel, locate the best shops and reasonably priced restaurants, find a tourist guide and information about museums and much more besides. For each of these things there are numerous sources of information, but often involving insecure data or confusing user interfaces.

A holiday is not just the time between getting on and off the plane or checking in and out of a hotel. A holiday typically has five stages. These begin with the initial idea and end with the slideshow on the flat-screen television in your living room. The holiday is a process that involves many aspects and therefore has to be planned in an integrated way: finding inspiration, searching, booking, travelling and then looking back on the journey all belong to a perfect holiday experience.

The best thing for most people would therefore be an integrated package of elements. However, the traditional package holiday, sold to millions of people in a more or less identical form, is becoming increasingly obsolete in a society where individualism is the growing trend. Not so our new 'carefree' travel package, because it is personalised for every individual customer. The comforting knowledge that a major travel brand has thought of and organised everything – i.e. the feel-good factor of the traditional package holiday – is something that customers still want to have.

And this is all about making the journey a success. Complete peace of mind without having to worry that something could go wrong. The perfect holiday!

To revolutionise the travel market you have

to turn it upside down, and create a market-place where all participants in the travel process can meet up.

Today, electronic travel booking involves data and more data. This data is lodged in so many different systems that the process of booking a trip is far from user friendly, despite the vast sums of money already invested in modernising everything. Unless, of course, a completely new system can be created, with structural data that is constantly updated and easy to access. Whether you're looking for that initial inspiration for the trip, or a particular tip on what to do during your stay, quality data will always be the focal point of the new marketplace.

All the providers who are responsible for a particular section of the journey – airlines, hotels, restaurants, bus companies etc. – will be highly motivated to feed in data on everything from descriptions of services to availability and capacity details. This reminds us of the app store, because all these companies will be able to work like app developers.

After going through quality control, this important data is lodged in one central location and can immediately be accessed by the holidaymaker. What's special about this is that *anyone* can take part. Not only large, long-established companies, but also small, family-run restaurants and boat hire firms can feed their information into the marketplace. Similar to the tools used by Apple app developers which helped to establish a billion-dollar market, the newly developed tools will be even more of a boon for this target group.

All the data will be systemised using the platform guidelines. Four stars in southern Europe will mean exactly the same as four stars in North America. If an offer promises a 'sea view', the quality control of the data will ensure that one sea view really is comparable with the others.

Travellers can now receive information about the different options open to them via a platform on the Net. For the inspiration phase, it won't be only the catalogue texts from travel operators that are available, but also information from independent tourist offices and travel guides. In particular, the possibility of using several professional sources simultaneously when planning a trip will open up new business models for publishers, such as the sale of various articles about travel destinations.

To give a clear overview of which destinations and hotels are particularly recommended, travellers will be asked to supply commentaries and ratings. The trick is that they will be automatically contacted while they are at the destination, via an app which acts as the traveller's constant companion. The big advantage is that the system only contains reviews written by the traveller at the place in question. Success guaranteed! In the same way, travellers are asked to supply any missing photos or updates from their trips.

A customer wanting to book a trip is first shown the basic options from which he or she can choose. The next stage shows a selection of bookable offers, tailored to the individual's personal preferences. These 'inspirations' may be based on the destination, time of travel, personal interests or cultural activities. The large number of inquiries the traveller has to make nowadays can be greatly reduced by the high-quality nature of the data, because all the information is included in a system optimised for travel bookings and not spread out on various servers throughout the Internet. In addition, instead of asking the user too many questions, the system makes particular assumptions. Every time customers use the system, it gets to know them better and can make more personalised suggestions and recommendations. Someone who has often travelled alone, for example, will not be offered family holidays, and is thus able quickly to access offers that address their own personal interests.

When the customer has booked a trip and arrived at the holiday destination, the app provides constantly updated support, thus adding to the positive holiday experience. A day planner makes informal suggestions showing times and costs. A bicycle tour can be booked at the touch of a virtual button. Data from cycle hire companies makes this possible, because the marketplace continues to act as a broker between the various market participants throughout the whole holiday.

The cycle hire company can be sure to get a reliable paying customer and the traveller knows that the cycle firm will take great care to offer service and quality. After all, during a short break, the system asks the traveller to rate the bikes and the service offered. And this can be the incentive for other tourists to use that particular cycle hire company.

If the traveller wishes, the photos and videos taken during the journey can be combined with the information gathered during the various phases of the trip to create a multimedia show. The names of the locations and descriptions of the activities shown are automatically included with the images. And if the owner of that amazing nightclub has fed the playlist into the system, it will even provide the right music for that part of the slideshow.

All the five stages of travel are displayed on an integrated platform which accompanies the traveller at every step, whether as an app or website. The customer therefore has personalised information at his or her disposal throughout the journey.

AN APPLE TOY SYSTEM

The toy market is a highly complex marketing and licensing business, offering products in increasingly rapid innovation cycles. Toys are part of a holistic strategy on the part of their manufacturers that reflects the everyday life of a child, from breakfast to dinner and from nursery to school. Strategies are usually designed for multiple channels and can involve new characters being promoted via a TV series in order to sell them as toy figures in toy shops and online in the form of digital games. One of the industry's major problems is an increasing shift of 'play time' towards digital media.

WHAT WOULD APPLE DO TO BECOME
A SUCCESSFUL MANUFACTURER
OF TOYS AND GAMES?

The first step is to ask what problems we, as adults, have with modern toys. Low-quality plastic products which frequently have to be replaced or enhanced tend to be unpopular with parents. Adults can easily lose track of the big picture, because there are an enormous number of items on offer, and it's hard to understand why a child wants a particular one. Parents who want to give their child a toy as a gift face a bewildering challenge: on the one hand they want to fulfil the child's wishes, but on the other, many of the toys of the moment don't appear to be particularly suitable for a child. For example, playing cards with medieval fantasy characters that deal with all kinds of magic and special powers and can be 'swapped', 'won' or 'lost' in a highly complex system fail to impress many parents.

The market is complex: the purchaser is often not the consumer and most suppliers are struggling to retain the interest of their target group. This is a prime example of a situation in which Apple's strategies can be applied very effectively.

To make toys and games attractive for a media-permeated society, you have to forget any romantic notions about wooden toys and analyse why children are fascinated by digital media. Why do many children prefer to play on a screen than with a model railway? What exactly is missing from most analogue toys?

The answer is interaction and networking. Although traditional toys are more conducive to creativity and are better learning aids, young people tend to be more enthusiastic about the new interactive possibilities available. Machines are the new toys – able to communicate with their users. Every action leads to a reaction and creates a feeling of power and control in the user. Interaction and networking can guarantee the success of digital games.

And then there's Lego: the building blocks that can be used to make almost anything. Lego has been enjoyed by generation after generation, because there's always something new to build and it encourages a pastime that parents favour for their children. Children also enjoy creative, productive toys, where they themselves are in charge. Taking inspiration from Lego and Apple, how should a modern toy be designed to make it captivating for parents and children alike?

The answer is a toy system, and is based on the assumption that children are naturally creative and still want to live this out in the age of the iPad and online social networks. Compared to the generations before them, they have the opportunity to unleash their own ideas and creations on the real world. The normal consumer can today get hold of a 3D printer for around £300. Our toy of the future will be available at an affordable price, specially produced en masse and subsidised by the manufacturer. The real show-stopper is the platform, not the product.

Building blocks, cups, containers, figures, glasses, masks, board games, mechanical devices and thousands of other things can be printed at home using a special plastic material. And these can be combined with existing toys and games.

You can either develop the ideas and structures yourself using a simple program on your PC, or upload a pattern for a figure or toy from the manufacturer's platform. On this platform you will find not only professional model figures from the latest films along with the accompanying accessories (all under licence), but also ideas and construction plans from other users. In future, profitable business will consist mostly of selling the basic building materials for the printer and developing ideas, which can be customised by children and their parents.

Children thus have the chance to discuss their toys on a secure platform. They can write about their building projects online using simple tools, or just brag about a new must-have figure they have printed. We're talking about a new social network based on toys and games, and one that does not exist only on a virtual level, because the 3D printer will bring everything to life.

Today's most popular branded model figures will remain big hits on the new platform. Many customers will download fee-based 3D figures from the worlds of Harry Potter, Star Wars, Cars and Donald Duck. But as in the app store, alongside the major brands there will be a huge number of smaller suppliers, harnessing their creativity and ideas to offer new characters, stories and models and thus satisfy customers' individual needs.

A great model is like a great app or a great computer game: it takes time, experience and creativity to develop it. That's why our new platform takes care of the sale *and* the legal protection of what is created. A 3D creation can only be downloaded and printed using the secure method offered by the operating company. Therefore a share of the sales is retained to refinance the platform.

Producers of computer games can ensure that real models of their toy characters and superheroes find their way into children's homes. Board game manufacturers can develop new concepts such as individual, personalised versions of Monopoly, Cluedo and other popular board games showing, for example, the faces of one's own family.

The secret of a good toy or game is to combine traditional values regarding play-things with the current fascination for technology to create products that children love and which parents can relate to.

Armed with a 3D printer, adults and older children can build all types of toys, whether well-known licensed characters or their own individual creations.

AN APPLE NEWSPAPER
PUBLISHER

In the publishing sector, people's opinions about Apple tend to differ. On the one side are those who are grateful to Apple for helping them make money with digital content for devices like the iPad. On the other are most publishing executives, who complain about having to share revenue with a large company. Revenue generated by their own content.

Wherever you stand in this debate, the question you have to ask remains:

WHAT WOULD APPLE DO TO ESTABLISH A SUCCESSFUL NEWSPAPER PUBLISHING COMPANY?

Today, most people want to access extremely up-to-date news on the Net for free. Nationwide news, world events and what's happening locally can be accessed without cost on all the relevant news portals. The competition is fierce, but at least the major newspaper brands seem to be able to refinance everything through the advertising revenue.

Apple creates products that are valued by customers and can therefore be offered for a fee. If digital news is not the best area to be in, then we shall have to explore other avenues.

People have been reading and enjoying newspapers since they were invented. Until the Internet starting putting pressure on this business model, they were willing to pay for this privilege.

But this pressure applies only to the distribution model, not to the articles on topics that interest people. To deliver a printed newspaper to people's letterboxes early every morning was a valuable logistical service in itself, together with the actual content. In the digital age this is no longer necessary, which robs publishers of a major USP.

People looking for information tend to use several sources. Newspaper brands still have a role to play, but this is less significant than it was in the print era. People tend to enjoy the feature pages of one paper, the excellent business section of another and the good coverage of local news in yet another. Many also read blogs on particular subjects.

But hardly anyone who is regularly on the Net will use just one newspaper brand or source.

So now we're going to develop a platform on which the well-known newspaper brands still play a role, but the writers themselves assume a far more important one. A platform with an abundance of authors that also ensures that individual articles are not only read but also purchased. An iTunes for articles, background information reports, editorial comments, dossiers and opinions, all in the form of a central newspaper platform, where the customers have to pay for every item. As the writers now play a more important role, good ideas and concepts supplied by freelance journalists have the same chance of becoming a commercial success as content from the major newspaper brands and their writers. And the customer can choose between a single purchase and various subscription options.

If customers like a particular author, they can subscribe to his articles. If they favour a particular newspaper brand and its content, a suitable subscription is also available. A customer can also access the entire platform for a flat rate. The authors and newspaper brands are then paid proportionately.

As with iTunes, you can group your favourite items in a playlist. A perfectly arranged collection of articles and information is then available on the device in question.

This new platform is not just about digital distribution; it's also about a new type of journalism that puts the authors in the spotlight and ensures that they get paid.

The new offering serves to group together the numerous texts and posts available today. Fashion bloggers, great critical minds focusing on home affairs, music lovers and local patriots: there are so many good writers and a wealth of good content. But today, most of this can be found somewhere on the Net for free, so freelance journalists and bloggers struggle to make a living from the limited proceeds. What's missing are the real crowd pullers, who usually work for major newspapers. But if all of them write for one platform, they can all profit from each other. Famous journalists have the chance to work alongside up-and-coming avant-garde writers. And freelancers – often specialist journalists – have the chance to get noticed in a marketplace where the great and famous are also present.

The platform has not only a rating and commentary function, but also a recommendation logic that allows content to be personalised. Similar to the Apple Genius feature, the user receives recommendations based on their preferences and articles read in the past.

The platform gets to know you and will make increasingly attractive and relevant offers the more you use it.

It goes without saying that the content can be accessed on all available devices. For example, a reader who leaves the house after reading his personalised morning paper on a tablet can continue to read it on the train to work using a smartphone. Once in the office, the PC knows which articles have not yet been read and displays these accordingly. On the journey back home, the reader can have the remaining articles read to him or listen to audio commentaries. In the evening he can then watch the content from the current issue on a TV set. This is possible because the content platform consistently uses the same system, retaining control over both the reader experience and, importantly, the underlying technology.

Authors are paid for the use of their content. Whether earned from subscribers or individual purchases, most of the proceeds go to the author. Individual writers can plan with a steady cash flow if people subscribe to their work, and those with a large number of subscribers will tend to put more effort into an article than writers who mostly sell their pieces on a one-off basis.

For special projects, the platform provides a funding market where journalistic ideas can be pitched. A writer who intends to cover the Arab Spring in Egypt will illustrate the concept and attempt to win the necessary funding from interested parties before the trip. If the funding campaign is successful, the report can proceed; if not, then no one has to pay anything. If, on the other hand, the report is successful, the investors can partake in the success, either in the form of money, or by getting access to exclusive content.

As well as being able to sell all types of content, the new newspaper platform also provides layout design for this content. Existing newspaper brands can thus ensure that their readers recognise their distinctive visual style, while other writers can make their offerings unmistakable with their own individual design and creative ideas. The system automatically ensures the compatibility of the various sources. Readers no longer have to wrestle with lots of different formats and technical details, but are able to sit back and enjoy the content that interests them.

Unlike Apple's app store, the new newspaper platform will only work in the absence of censorship. Freedom of the press must remain unchallenged, regardless of modern concepts and new ideas.

A content platform provides for all aspects of added value in journalism, so that newspaper brands, authors and readers have a common marketplace in which they can find one another.

EPILOGUE

The post-PC era – heralded by Apple's launch of the iPad in 2010 – changed the way in which people interact with computers. Since then, the idea of apps has also become more and more important, not just for Apple but in general. In the PC era, software was carefully installed, updated on a regular basis and studied in books and seminars. Apps are different: they are tiny, often have a single purpose and just a few important functions, and can almost always be used without any training.

Apps are like chocolate bars that people take with them when they are travelling. They are no longer investment goods, but rather

off-the-shelf products. Studies regarding
the use of apps on the iPhone have shown
that people tend to purchase individual apps
precisely at the moment when they need
them and when they are in vogue. After a few
months, many of them are no longer in use,
either because they did not really deliver, or
because better ones have become available.
So we see that people today are willing to buy
software and discard it after a while.

If someone is in the middle of decorating
the house, and realises that he needs a spirit
level, he no longer needs to drive to a hardware store, but can download an app from the
app store in seconds, all the while standing on
the ladder. Most people probably don't care
whether this spirit level app costs fifty pence
or £1.50; if they need something immediately,
they are normally willing to pay for it.

So, a new understanding of technology has
emerged, with the large-scale comprehensive solutions of the past twenty years being
gradually replaced with focused, compact
applications, each for a specific purpose.

Furthermore, apps put complicated and some-times inaccessible Internet offerings into small, convenient packages. The phenomenon of shopping with a smartphone is currently undergoing a revolution, not because of new products that are available, but because apps are making it easier than ever to shop.

Anyone hoping to sell digital products or services should ask themselves how custom-ers are using their product. Is it possible to translate large software packages to much smaller, more convenient apps that can be offered to the customer at the right time and the right place? The platforms for doing this already exist. Anyone who runs a website should ask themselves how they can pick out the key functions and package them in the form of apps.

DEVELOPMENTS IN THE POST-PC ERA

Developing apps is an entirely new discipline. By introducing touchscreens and dispensing with the keyboard and mouse for the iPod, iPhone and iPad, Apple redefined the job of the industry designer, with screen design now being of central importance. Developing graphical user interfaces has become an essential part of product development.

Screen design is also a new discipline, which contributes enormously to the success of a digital product. Leaving out control elements, such as the keyboard, that were connected to the hardware was nothing less than a revolution, the effects of which are still not foreseeable. From a graphical point of view, the days when programs like Word were developed for PCs or Macs and the basic interface metaphors and interaction patterns emerged will have almost nothing in common with the world of tomorrow.

Designing touchscreens obviously requires a thorough knowledge of graphic design and typography. It is, however, also important that a screen designer understands what Dieter Rams and his colleagues did forty years ago, because the rules of good design are as valid today as they were then. The fact that the keys and buttons of digital gadgets are situated beneath a sheet of glass means that products like the iPhone and iPad are versatile, universal devices. With the right app, they can turn into practically any 'thing' you want – a pocket calculator, a spirit level, a camera, a telephone or a marble run.

Whereas in the past many industry designers working with actual materials were needed, today a developer can create products that at least *appear* to be real, just using lines of code.

The quality of virtual devices is, however, still determined by the standard of their design – just as it was for actual products sixty years ago. Whereas people used to carry real objects to the patent office to protect a particular design or feature, today, protection is required for virtual design concepts. Not until 2010 did Apple patent the hand gesture used to unlock the iPhone: the movement made by the finger to slide the virtual button to the right. Remember, this is a button that does not really exist.

No one who wants to develop digital

products will be able to avoid the new inter-face metaphors, interaction patterns and concepts. And it will not be possible simply to rely on web standards, because the touch-screen interfaces require completely new input methods. A user who, for example, no longer has a mouse in hand and has to use her fingers will not be thrilled if she has to touch tiny words on the screen of the iPad in order to navigate. This is why the hand gestures and interfaces for iPads have since been integrated into the design of websites. Larger keys, large-format images and an extremely simple navigation structure are now essential, because it is known from the start that users will also surf the website using iPads.

THE NEW DESIGN

Following the death of Steve Jobs, Apple's new CEO, Tim Cook, reorganised the mobile team. Scott Forstall, Jobs's long-time companion and head of the department responsible for the iOS mobile operating system, left Apple, and Cook transferred his duties to product designer Jonathan Ive. Many regarded this as an important step to strengthen Apple's innovative power. Forstall and Jobs paved the way for the post-PC era, borrowing many design features from actual objects such as leather-bound address books and cases – something known as 'skeuomorphism'. They also created one of the best mobile operating systems, now widely available and well established.

The current responsibilities of Jony Ive mean that an Apple product designer is now responsible not only for hardware, but also for the virtual buttons and keys created by code. This step demonstrates that devices like the iPhone and the iPad have taken on a new role: smartphones and tablets are now 'meta-objects' that can be transformed into hundreds and thousands of things with the help of apps.

HOW TO EARN DIGITAL MONEY

We have seen that Apple is not only a model for numerous companies that develop useful digital products and services and want to earn money with them. Apple is also the direct manufacturer and operator of platforms that have heralded a new era for digital business models. The post-PC era is post-PC largely thanks to the app store. Here everyone, big or small, can sell their products and services to millions of people who have got used to the fact that software, journalistic content and other apps cost money. Millions of people are now willing to spend money on digital products.

Anyone who poses the question 'What's in it for *me*?' is advised to spend a day looking at the many apps that can now be purchased in the app store. It doesn't take long to get an idea of the enormous number and variety of apps available, mostly created by small-scale app developers. There are countless success stories which were made possible by the infrastructure provided by Apple. Today, many start-ups prefer to put all their efforts into an app, instead of taking an 'indirect route' via a website. Projects such as Instagram, Path and Fab are good examples of how new business models can emerge with the help of the platforms of the post-PC era.

Apple has developed and successfully marketed numerous revolutionary products, from the first Macintosh to the iPhone 5, from those colourful iMacs to the iPod and, most recently, the iPad – ushering in the post-PC era. Apple has laid the foundations of the digital future and is the pioneer of modern digital product development. However, digitalisation will clearly continue to change the world, and new issues will come to the fore.

Will the users of Facebook, Google and similar platforms be willing, in the long run, to make their personal data permanently available in exchange for free programs and services? What if people decide that they no longer want to be mere data in a system and simply unsubscribe? How would digital advertising develop if it were no longer able to base its activities on the interests and characteristics of the user, because states intervened to regulate data collection or because users objected to the lack of privacy? Apple's mindset, as we have seen, can be likened to that of a traditional medium-sized company.

It's all about quality, utility and innovation. However, a mindset like this also involves having the self-confidence to demand money for one's products: *real* money paid directly by the customers, not by giving certain products their attention, or by surrendering their right to privacy. The product has to stand up for itself and people have to pay for it.

Since his death, almost everything has already been said about the person of Steve Jobs. But he has left something behind. Anyone who is looking for ways to be success-ful in the digital world can look to his life's work – Apple – as inspiration. The potential generated by that unique mindset, the radical development model and the world-famous communication policy can be harnessed by anyone who wants to create their own work of art and make money in the digital world.

THANKS

The author wishes to thank Sabrina, Carsten, Ramona, Jürgen, Sam, Paul, Hannah, Ella, Tanja, Sille, Christopher, Bene, Tom, Hans, Heiner, David, Mark, Nicola and Bernd.

ABOUT THE AUTHOR

Dirk Beckmann, born in 1969 in Gelsenkirchen, Germany, is an entrepreneur, author and lecturer. The main subjects of his work are digital business models, new technology and Design Thinking.

While studying economics in 1991 he founded the digital communication agency artundweise where, as managing director, he is responsible for customers including Kraft Foods, Kellogg's, Mars and other well-known German and international companies.

The German edition of this book was nominated for the German Business Book Award 2011.

He teaches 'Marketing in the Digital Age' at Bremen University and lectures at numerous congresses and events.